HEAVEN SENT

Heaven Sent

A True Story of Losing Hope and Finding an Angel

Jerry Loye Crawley

outskirts press

Heaven Sent
A True Story of Losing Hope and Finding an Angel

v4.0

Outskirts Press, Inc.
http://www.outskirtspress.com

ISBN: 978-1-9772-3161-1

PRINTED IN THE UNITED STATES OF AMERICA

WRITTEN FOR AYDEN

September 26, 1999 – November 1, 2008

Inspired by memories that will never fade
And a love that will never die.

Acknowledgment

Which of the many thousands of people, who have entered and exited your life, do you thank after you've written your first book? That's a really good question for which I'm not sure I have an adequate answer.

So, I'll start by making a list my parents, Loye Long and Dora Sue Poteat Crawley, would definitely be at the top of. After all, they're the ones who furnished me the moral compass that helped head me in the right direction, after leaving their loving home… and always pointed true north when I would need a change of course, after many instances of losing my way. My only regret is, they're no longer here for me to thank in person, but I'm sure they know.

Then, there's my brother, Alvin Lee, whom I still love, even after "butting heads" with him on numerous occasions…which I'm positive resulted in him no longer feeling the same about me. And my sister, Joan Phyllis Nile, whom I've butted heads with an equal number of times, but never stopped loving me…and never will.

I also want to thank my estranged wife, Sandra, who after forty years, finally gave up the struggle, but never stopped caring. And my three children; Nathan, Adrian and Lorrinda, who have always been there to push, prod, pull and prop me up.

I was blessed with nine grandchildren; M'Lynn, Andrew, Keegan, A'lyssa, Jordan, Jace, Jammer and Molli, who love me in spite of my many faults, omissions and short-comings. And Ayden, who listened intently to all of my stories about Shep, then left Heaven's portals just long enough to goad me into writing about them.

I'd be remiss if I failed to mention the people who helped make it technically possible for me to write this book. These include my fine English teachers from high school, Mrs. Nina Lafevers and Mrs. Lena Taylor, who contributed tremendously to the knowledge required to author a book that would be readable. And Beverly Hyatt, Annelle Mulwee and Mary Rasnick, who graciously edited it for me, to make sure it was. And Libby Bridges, who was there at the start of this project to provide me with any materials, resources and answers I lacked…as well as encouragement when I became discouraged.

And just so I don't leave anyone out who may, or may not, have lent a hand in making the writing of this book a reality, let me take this opportunity to thank my extended family members, as well as the myriad of people who have befriended me throughout my life. For many of you contributed vital and significant experiences, both positive and negative, that helped form my open-minded attitude and non-judgmental convictions, thereby adding value and worth in the molding of the soul of this writer. I can't name all of you, but I'm sure you know who you are.

For the sake of thoroughness, I also want to thank anyone

who may have disliked me and took glee, or simply showed apathy, during a few instances when my demise appeared imminent, if for no other reason than providing me the added incentive of proving them wrong.

Most importantly, I would like to use this opportunity to thank my Creator for impeding my life with the hardships and struggles I was forced to contend with, during the period this book was written about, as well as some times more recent. Then, bestowing in me the determination to overcome them, the presence of mind to finally recognize them for what they were, the wisdom to transform them into lessons learned, and the talent to later record them for posterity.

As in my book, just when I reached the end of this long, but necessary, acknowledgment, the answer to the question asked at the beginning of it hit me square in the face. Which of the vast multitude of people, who have played a role in your life, do you thank after writing a book? You thank them all.

Table of Contents

Prologue

This is the true story of a boy and his dog reconstructed from my memories at ages five through nine. Nothing is exaggerated or sensationalized, and I took no artistic license in describing any events which occur in this book. Although many of the episodes depicted may seem extraordinary to some, dogs have been astounding man from the time the first wolves gazed into his campfire light.

While all of the events described in my story are factual, I was, however, unable to remember some of the depictions and much of the dialog verbatim, because of my age at the time and the many years that have passed since they occurred. Therefore, I closed the missing gaps to the best of my recollection, or as I perceived it to have happened.

So before the destructive forces of time rob me of any more of these precious memories, I'm, at last, putting pen to paper to document the extraordinary life of an animal whose exploits of love, devotion and courage, during his short stay on this earth, merit their reclamation from obscurity. A mysterious life in which its very purpose for existing exceeds much of human understanding.

Heaven and Heartbreak

I don't remember who saw him first, my dad or me. After all, sixty-five years can really play havoc on the memory of an old man who has problems recollecting even more current events. And it may actually not seem all that long ago to most adults who've had the good fortune to live well into their sixties and seventies. However, when you're attempting to dredge up enough old memories, from that deep into your past, to write a book, you might as well be speaking in terms of light years. But as odd as it may seem, that's about the only part of the little pup's life I have the least bit of difficulty remembering.

I even recall telling my father that the mostly Collie pup curled up in a ball in the corner of our house foundation and chimney, on a cold November morning, was the most beautiful thing I'd ever seen. Evidently, Dad had a similar reaction to the little guy. Of course, it may have just been pity for the tiny ball of fur, trying to catch what little heat he could radiating from the bricks. But regardless, when I asked if we could keep him, to my astonishment, he replied in the affirmative.

I think it was something like, "Yeah, I suppose so, unless he belongs to somebody, and they come to claim him."

What made it surprising was the fact that Dad already owned eight beagles, which he used for his passion, rabbit hunting. And they weren't cheap to feed for a family man who worked the "graveyard" shift in a local textile mill, with three kids and a stay-at-home wife.

But, anyway, that was good enough for me. Trying to contain my joy, I reached down to pick him up. When he opened his eyes and looked into mine for the first time, it was love at first sight. At least, it was for me.

The next order of business was coming up with a suitable name for the newest addition to our family. When I couldn't think of one off the top of my head, other than maybe, *Fido* or *Spot*...neither of which seemed all that appropriate...I asked Dad what he thought.

He appeared to mull it over in his head for a few seconds, before suggesting, "How 'bout, *Shep*?"

I didn't know where in creation he had come up with that name, but it sounded absolutely perfect to this six year-old boy... simple, but at the same time, majestic! It wasn't until several years later that I learned he got it from a song recorded by Red Foley in 1946 titled, *Old Shep*.

Even though Dad had warned me that the pup may belong to someone, as far as I was concerned, from that moment on, he was mine. The little sable and white fur ball cradled in my arms was now my Shep, and I wasn't about to allow myself to even consider the possibility of him belonging to someone else. Besides, I thought, even if he had gotten lost or ran away, it was now a matter of "finders, keepers." At least, that's what I'd always been told. However, I preferred to believe that maybe someone no longer wanted him, and had set him out on the side of the road, where he just happened to stop to rest at our house.

Yeah, that could've been exactly what happened! Anyway, that's what I was going to believe. Someone had put the little fellow out because they ended up with a litter of puppies they didn't want. Heck, he could even have some brothers and sisters wandering around nearby that were homeless, too.

But I couldn't allow myself to worry about anything like that...not now, anyway. I had just experienced the worst nightmare imaginable, the previous summer, and was still struggling with the after effects of it. So what I needed more than anything, at this juncture in my life, was a friend...and what a friend I just knew he was going to be!

Sure, I had my younger brother, Alvin and my older sister, Joan. But they were just that, my brother and sister. What I longed for most, was a close companion...a really good buddy that would constantly hang around me. Someone who would always listen patiently and attentively when I told him about my problems and troubles. And boy, did I have a lot of problems and troubles to tell him about. Especially, after that terrible summer I had just endured...well, the second half of it, anyway.

Now, I know exactly what you're thinking. How could a five year-old boy...I didn't turn six until November 1st...have a summer so dreadful that it would still be bothering him all the way into late autumn? But I don't want to get ahead of myself, so I'll have to explain all that a little later. Right now, it's just about a kid and a pup.

I don't think I let Shep out of my sight the rest of that day, except, of course, when my mom would call me in for meals. That evening, after supper, I tried to sneak a biscuit out to him, but Dad's keen eye saw what I was up to and put a stop to it. He said we shouldn't start feeding him until we checked with the neighbors to see if anyone had lost a pup. So I couldn't help but smile, a little later that day, when Dad was making his way down to the beagle enclosure with his bucket of dry dog feed mixed with our table scraps. When he noticed Shep trailing along hungrily behind him, he stopped and put a scoop of it on the ground.

That night, when it was time for me to come inside and get ready for bed, I knew it would be a hopeless endeavor to ask Mom and Dad if it would be okay for Shep to come in, too. Dogs just weren't "inside folks" in that household. So when I was finally tucked away in my bed, nice and warm, it was all I could do to fall asleep, thinking of the little fellow lying outside in the cold.

Apparently, my father had felt some compassion for him, also. When I awoke the following morning and ran out to check on him, I saw where Dad had placed an old door mat on the front porch for Shep to lay on. I moved it in front of the bedroom window I shared with my four year-old brother, so I would be able to look out and see him. Little did I realize, this would be Shep's bed for the remainder of his life…just a small rug exposed to the harsh winter winds and blowing rain, sleet and snow. But even on the coldest nights, with any one of these harsh elements raging around him, he never once left his post.

When he saw me come out to greet him that first morning, you couldn't imagine a happier little guy. With his tail wagging furiously, he began jumping up and down, all the while letting go the most beautiful little bark I had ever heard…even to this day. When I knelt down to take him in my arms, he began licking my face, as if to let me know how much he had missed me.

Throughout the following days, Shep and I were constantly together. Whether rolling around in the front yard, playing in the woods and fields behind our home or just sitting on the front porch swing with him in my arms, we were inseparable. And when Mom would call me in for meals, or at bedtime, Shep would just stare, longingly, at the door for several minutes, before finally lying down on his mat.

At the beginning of it, I thought it would be just one more glorious, carefree day spent playing with Shep, like the twelve or so since our first meeting. But this one began to "go south," pretty quickly, after I noticed the Haskin sisters walking down the road in our direction. Then the hairs on the back of my neck stood straight up when Betty, the younger of the two, said to Mule, "It had to be him! I'm sure of it!"

I know you're already thinking, "*Mule?*" But yes, that was her name…well, her nickname, anyway. And like me, at that time, I'm sure you're also wondering what would lead a father, mother, sister…or anyone, for that matter…to nickname a girl *Mule*? And why would a fourteen year-old girl even go along with it, when she had such a nice, simple given name like *Nancy*?

It could've been she was given this unusual nickname because she had always been rather large for her age, or maybe the girl was just overly stubborn. But whatever the reason, I never really gave it that much thought after hearing her called it a few times. After all, my father had started calling me "Butch" before I was even able to walk. And I had a nice, simple given name, also…*Jerry.*

Anyhow, here they came, talking excitedly to each other as they approached our driveway. Hopefully, they would do as they always did when walking down the road in the direction of our house…keep on going to the next one, the house the Greene sisters, Johnsie and Ozelle, lived in. Now, if a couple girls could use a nickname, it was those two.

But no, they were turning in to our driveway! My first impulse was to grab Shep and run…or maybe I could hide him! No, it was already too late for that. Suddenly, one of the girls, I don't remember which, screamed, "Jimmy!" at the top of her lungs, when she saw Shep staring at them from between my legs. Then, both of them began screaming, "Jimmy!" while running full speed in our direction. And to make matters worse, Shep began running toward them!

Mom, hearing all the commotion taking place in our front yard, came running out the front door with my sister close behind. I don't remember if Dad, who was still in bed after working third shift the previous night, came out or not. To be honest, I was too stunned and numb to remember much of anything after that. All I could think was, "Betty and Mule are coming to take my pup!"

I do think I remember Betty saying something like, "I thought that looked like Jimmy on your front porch yesterday, when I was on my way back from Johnsie's house. So I thought I'd bring Mule back with me today, to make sure…and that's him! Daddy bought him at a kennel, somewhere up in the mountains, for my birthday present."

By that time, Shep had run back between my legs and was just staring at them again. Then, I remember looking up at Mom when Mule asked if they owed us anything for his board. Mom just looked pitifully down at me while simply answering, "No."

I knew what she was thinking, so I reached down and picked Shep up, then handed him to Betty. After that, I ran as fast as I could to my bedroom, because that was all I could think to do at the time. And I sure as heck wasn't going to just stand there and let those girls see me cry!

I don't remember much after that…just Mom opening my door and saying, "I'm sorry." And Joan coming in and sitting down at the foot of my bed, and sobbing. She loved the little guy, too, but nothing like I did. Alvin…well, at four, was just too young to understand.

Anyway, there I was…lying on my bed, too heartbroken to cry, with my sister doing enough for both of us. My little world had come crashing down around me again, and I knew all of my horrible nightmares would soon return. I may as well have been back in that awful hospital bed in Asheville, with strange people coming in at all hours of the night, and weird sounds constantly filling my ears…and my mom and dad fifty miles away.

Just when my world was starting to turn happy again, and I no longer dreaded the sound of Dad's car coming up the driveway in the mornings…this happens. What could a six year-old boy have possibly done for God to punish him so harshly? Why couldn't my life be like the ones of the other kids I knew? Why couldn't I just have normal things happen to me, like everyone else? And why in the heck would anyone name a dog, *Jimmy*?

The Emergency

From what I can recall of my life prior to the summer of 1954, everything seemed normal to me. However, being only five years old at the time, I hadn't had enough life experiences to know what normal was…and compared to what? I'm not even sure how our economic status would be defined, in regard to the other families living on that winding stretch of country road, in the foothills of western North Carolina.

Socially and economically speaking, I know we were probably somewhere in the middle compared to most of the other folks living there. But there were a few families who were so impoverished that it had to have lowered the bar quite a bit, when measured against most other Burke County neighborhoods. So, with that being the case, I'll just say that my family was somewhere between lower middle class and upper poor.

However, we did live in a newly constructed house my father built, nail by nail and board by board, with only the help of a seventeen year-old kid, who lived about a half mile from us.

Remarkably, Dad didn't owe anything on our new home when it was completed in 1947, about a year before I was born. He paid for it with his withheld combat pay, earned by dodging bullets and shell fragments, while serving in World War II as a medic.

Although Dad never had to worry about a mortgage hanging over his head, he did, unfortunately, run out of money before adding a few things that most people today would undoubtedly consider necessary conveniences. We didn't have electricity run to the house until about three or four years after it was completed. I still remember the kerosene lamps we used for lighting, and the two wood-burning stoves…one for heating the house and the other for cooking our meals.

And how could I ever forget that old homemade icebox that passed for a refrigerator. Using hand-hewn, white pine boards, Dad constructed a large chest, with both inner and outer walls. He then filled the space between the walls with sawdust to provide insulation. Then, to prevent leakage when the ice inevitably melted, he lined the inner surface with rubber obtained from old tire inner tubes. This was a prime example of the "hillbilly engineering" still practiced during that era in some of the more remote locales. Folks born just a decade later will never witness anything like it again, in this country. But if they do, I sure hope they're living in a well-constructed cave, deep inside a mountain!

It was another five years before Dad could afford to have the house plumbed for running water, but, sadly, that didn't include a bathroom. However, he did install a shower in the half-basement, which we used during the warmer months, and occasionally during the winter…well, only if we were full of enough "grit and vinegar," as there was no heat down there.

Dad finally got around to adding the bathroom when I was

fourteen. I think I carried around the stigma, for years afterward, of being one of the last kids in my circle of friends who still had to use an outdoor toilet. But Mamma always told me; what doesn't kill you, will only make you stronger. If that had actually been true, it was probably a good thing I never crossed paths with Superman during that period of my life. Because if he'd just looked at me the wrong way, I would've stomped a mud puddle in his butt!

I hope you readers don't mind the humor I'm trying to inject into the early chapters of this book, because a few of the later ones are actually downright depressing.

But anyway, that's just the way my father was, frugal and tight with his money...although that may not be a fair representation, considering what little he had. But suffice it to say, Dad never looked too kindly at putting his new house and eleven acres of land on hock to some bank, just to add on a few "conveniences." Especially, if he thought he'd be able to do it somewhere down the road, without having to go in debt. Now, I'm sure I failed to appreciate my father's economic expertise at the time, but looking back on it today, wouldn't it be great if more people were that frugal and prudent with their money…and in the government's case, *ours*?

Regardless, I know it had to be really hard on my mother, rearing three children without what would be considered, even back then, standard household necessities…appliances and amenities most mothers today take for granted and give very little thought to. But at our tender ages, we kids didn't know the difference. To us, everything appeared commonplace, and our lives seemed to be rolling along just fine. Well, that is until that hot and humid day in early August of 1954…and only for me.

It started out just like any other day, until late that afternoon when I became very ill. A month or so prior, I'd had a tonsillectomy, but my condition appeared to have returned to normal by this time. So, no one connected the two episodes, and believed them to be totally isolated occurrences. However, we later learned that that was one of the ways it was spread... through the use of surgical instruments and utensils that hadn't been adequately sanitized. And I'm now certain, that's how I ended up contracting it.

I remember running and playing just like normal, at the beginning of the day. Then, later on, I suddenly began to feel weak and excessively tired. After going inside to lie down, I then developed a severe headache. Mom gave me an aspirin, and was confident I would soon be okay. After all, I had always been your typical, healthy, strapping young boy...one that had never been sick a lot. I even thought it would be like one of those tummy aches I got from time to time, and everything would eventually be fine. I was just going to have to tough it out.

However, when I awoke the following morning, after just a few hours of fitful sleep, I felt even worse. When Mom gave me another aspirin, I couldn't even get it to go down...or the water, for that matter. It wasn't that my throat was sore like it had been with the tonsillitis, this was completely different. It was as though my "swallower" wouldn't work, no matter how hard I tried!

Well, that was enough for Mom! With a worried look, she told Dad I needed to see Dr. Miller, right away. He was our family physician in the little town of Marion, about twelve miles west of where we lived. And boy, that was the last thing I wanted to hear. I had already spent way more time with him than I cared to, because of the tonsil problem. So, as you can imagine, marching my little butt into his office this soon afterward, wasn't scoring all that high on my bucket list. Now, it wasn't that I was afraid, mind you. It was just that he was always sticking things down my throat, causing me to gag. And man, I just haaaated to gag! Of course, after reaching my "golden" years, I've had doctors stick things in a lot worse places, causing even more painful reactions…but at five years of age, that was plenty bad enough.

However, by the time we reached Dr. Miller's office, I didn't care what he did to me, as long as he made me feel better. But when he finished thoroughly looking me over, without any of his silly attempts at making me laugh, I was pretty certain that wasn't going to be a viable option.

I remember him walking out of the examination room to talk to my parents, without having said a word to me. Then, the next thing I knew, I'm being wrapped up in blankets like a mummy, and loaded onto a stretcher. When a couple nurses rolled me out to the parking area behind the building, I was even more perplexed. But fortunately, Mom came running to me and put her hand on my head. When I asked her what was going on, she told me we were waiting on an ambulance. Then, I was going to be taken to a hospital in Asheville for some more tests.

Upon hearing this, I didn't think I was going to get the words out of my mouth fast enough, when I asked if she were coming, too. When she answered, "Of course, I am!" it made me feel a little less apprehensive. I'd always wanted to ride in one of those things, but sitting upright in the front seat…not lying stretched out in the rear.

I can just imagine the terrified look on my face when they slammed the gurney, with me in it, into the back. Thank God,

Mom was in there with me! When we sped out of the parking lot and onto the main highway, with the siren blaring, I just thought to myself, "Butch, what in the heck have you gotten yourself into, this time?"

The Hospital

It only took about an hour to make the trip over the Black Mountains to the small city of Asheville, but that had to have been the longest hour of my young life. The nurses in Marion had wrapped me so tightly in the two or three blankets, I was barely able to breathe. Then, to make matters worse, I was running a very high fever which caused me to sweat profusely. So if you're guessing this wasn't your typical Sunday drive through the mountains, then you're bordering on Nostradamus-like genius.

As soon as we arrived at the hospital, I was rushed to an operating room and laid face down on the surgical table. The next thing I remember, was a sharp, excruciating pain emanating from my lower back. You better believe I was screaming pretty loud, as Mom held on tightly to my arms while offering encouragement. But when I looked up at her and noticed she was crying almost as much as me, her words began to lose much of their soothing effect. Then, when I glanced down at the other end of the table and noticed a nurse holding my legs, I began scanning the room for my father. When I saw him holding up the wall behind him, displaying only a slight hint of concern, I began to realize that I may be pretty much on my own with this deal.

What I eventually learned, was that this was a spinal tap procedure, or lumbar puncture, designed to draw spinal fluid from between my lower vertebrae. It was essential that this was performed without the use of anesthesia to deaden the pain, so as to prevent any contamination to the specimen. The fluid was then sent to a lab for analysis, to determine if any infection was occurring within my central nervous system. When the diagnosis was finally completed, the doctors confirmed what Dr. Miller had suspected a few hours earlier…I had polio.

Poliomyelitis, also known as infantile paralysis, had spread more quickly than normal, mostly among young children, following the end of World War II…just as Spanish influenza had at the close of the First World War. Dr. Jonas Salk would develop a vaccine in 1952, which would prove successful in immunizing against this terrible disease. However, the vaccine wouldn't be widely available until the autumn of 1954, a few weeks after I had contracted it.

Do any of you readers need me to pick a horse for you at Pimlico…or how about a Powerball ticket at the local Seven-Eleven? I didn't think so.

When the nurses finally rolled me off the table, I was hoping that would be the end of it…that they would give me a couple aspirins, or something, then send me back home. Some of you may need to google the word, *naïve,* before you read any further.

As you've probably guessed by now, this was only the beginning of my problems. The next thing I knew, I was being taken to nearby Asheville Orthopedic Hospital, and things only got worse from there. Once I stupidly allowed myself to be admitted, they then hit me with the cold, hard facts. Neither Mom nor Dad would be staying there with me, so this wasn't going to be anything like my time at the hospital in Marion, a couple months earlier. There, my mother was with me for most of my three-day stay. No, sir! This time, it would only be the three of us; me, myself and Irene...and Irene had a wicked little grin on her face!

In fact, my parents had to leave almost immediately, and couldn't return until the following Sunday! And Sunday was the only day allowed for visitation! And visitation only lasted for two hours! Whew! Is it any wonder that the first thing I did after being put in my bed, was to look around for a means of escape?

I can't begin to describe to you just how horrible the remainder of that evening was, after my parents had left...as well as the succeeding mornings, afternoons and nights. But, hey...if you guys are game, then I'll give it a try.

I was placed in a ward with about twenty other boys, all close to my age. We each had our own bed, enclosed in metal railings which were about three feet high. On one side was a section that slid up and down on tracks, for getting in and out. However, I soon realized that the main purpose of this door was to keep you in. The beds were laid out in pairs, with a large metal cabinet placed between the two. The cabinet had a door on each side that allowed the corresponding bed occupant accessibility...but only if you asked a nurse. This is where we kept our personal items, such as pajamas, underwear and tooth brushes.

At one end of the spacious dormitory was a large bathroom for all of us to use, but only for bathing. When we needed to use the toilet, it was done in a bed pan, when requested from one of the three nurses on duty...with her looking on while you performed this vital, necessary and *personal* function. I very quickly realized this wasn't going to be one of those settings that pandered to the preferences of the shy and modest…which I happened to be both. I'm absolutely certain that's why, to this day, I'm still "pee shy" when using a public urinal.

At the other end of the large room were two rows of about twenty chairs. And they were all facing something that caused me to do a double-take when I first saw it. If any of you guessed a television set, then you win a cardboard cookie.

A television! I couldn't believe it! I bet you can tell by my excitement that we didn't own one. Although the TV wasn't playing when I first noticed it, I must have sat there and stared at the blank screen for thirty minutes. To my extreme consternation, I later learned that it was only turned on for two hours in the evenings, I think between the hours of five and seven. However, you were only allowed out of your bed to watch it, if you had been good that day.

By "good," I mean; eating all of your meals, and that means everything on your plate…not crying, even though you're so homesick you could walk all the way there in a cold rain…not talking excessively, which I was pretty good at, unless, of course, it was to myself…taking your medicines without spitting or gaging, including the warm prune juice they brought you at bedtime… and you could set your watch by it!

You heard me, warm prune juice! I still have nightmares about having my nose held shut while it's being forced down my throat. Even today, when I go to the grocery store, I try to avoid the aisle the stuff's on. I guess you've probably figured out by now that I didn't get to do a whole lot of TV viewing, during my stay there.

But the few times I did, I was hoping a western would be

playing…or a "cowboy show," as I referred to them back then. But who am I kidding? No more than I was allowed to watch the dang thing, I would've sat and stared at the test pattern…simply for the fact that it had an Indian on it!

About half way down the ward, and opposite the side the windows were on, was a large, ominous looking door…which, by the way, just happened to be next to my bed. No one was allowed to enter that room, other than the nurses, and it was usually kept locked…usually. However, I did just happen to "wander" inside there on one occasion, to very bad consequences. But I'll get around to telling about that a little later. I just wanted you to keep it in mind, until the time comes. This is a little trick my writing coach taught me, to build suspense. It cost me a lot of money to take that class, so I sure didn't want to write an entire book without incorporating something into it that I learned there.

I know you may not believe this, but I found some of the nurses to be somewhat less than congenial, and a few of them down right ornery! And I don't know if they were actually nurses, or just "glorified" attendants. But whatever they were, after only a few days in that abysmal place, I was certain they had all been put through some type of special training, or "boot camp," to instruct them in the fine art of being cruel to little children.

My first experience with this type of conduct was my second day there, when I witnessed a little boy being spanked for a relatively minor offense. Of course, I realize it was a different time and culture back then, and corporal punishment was very common, even in grade school. But this was a hospital…one that treated little, sick children, for crying out loud! I'm sorry, I didn't mean to lose my temper, but I still want to let go a "war whoop" whenever I think back on it. And that's probably because it wasn't a day or two later that yours truly, "moi," got a taste of this deplorable behavior.

We were taken from our beds for our evening meal, just as the food was being brought in on carts and placed on several small tables in the dining area. After reaching my chair, I looked apprehensively at the tray of food sitting in front of me. I knew I would have to eat it all, so I didn't want to be caught completely off guard by something I wasn't familiar with…and there it was!

The first thing this "beans and taters" country boy thought of when I looked down at the rather large helping sitting squarely in the center of my plate, was freshly gathered maggots from a recent roadkill, slowly simmered in a thick broth of rancid rat blood. If any of you readers are presently munching on nachos, or getting ready to eat dinner, then I sincerely apologize.

It turns out what I was actually being asked to eat, for the first time, was Spanish rice. But heck, who was I kidding? It might as well have been my original description, as far as I was concerned. And one other thing I probably need to clarify while I'm at it…I wasn't asked, I was told!

"What's this?" I meekly implored one of the nurses, while jabbing my spoon into the middle of the steaming pile of…well, you know what I'm talking about.

"Oh my! It seems we have one here that didn't get a menu." the nurse amusingly replied, with the other servers bursting into laughter.

"It's rice. Enjoy!" she finally answered, after wiping the stupid grin off her face.

"Rice?" I thought to myself. "Boy, it sure don't look like any rice I've ever eaten before. And certainly not the way Mom serves it to us, with sugar and butter."

Looking around the table at the sad faces of the other kids reluctantly forcing it down, made me even more determined to figure out a way to avoid the same, sad fate…but how?

"I know!" I thought. "I'll pull that old trick I use at home when I don't want to eat something. The one where I wait until no one is looking, then scrape it off into my brother or sister's plate."

However, I must've aroused the suspicion of the nurse I'd asked the question to, because she barely took her eyes off of me…and definitely not long enough to pull a stunt like that. But, fortunately, she did turn her head just long enough for me to throw my napkin over it. I then quickly ate the other items on my plate, drank my carton of milk, then sat there, politely, waiting for her to, hopefully, return me to my bed.

"Well, it looks like someone doesn't appreciate the "cuisine" here," the nurse said, after walking up behind me and removing the napkin.

"You have exactly two minutes to eat that," she demanded, while glancing at her watch.

I just looked down at the Spanish rice, then pitifully back up at her, while slowly shaking my head. What followed next, was a scene straight out of a Charles Dickens novel.

The nurse grabbed me by the nose, while forcing my head back. When I was no longer able to breathe, and had to open my mouth, she forced spoonful after spoonful of the rice into it. She then dropped the spoon and held her hand over my mouth, until I had no other option but to swallow. However, when she removed her hand, I spit what rice I hadn't swallowed back into the plate. Unfortunately, this only made her angry and even more determined to get the rice inside of me. Gritting her teeth, the nurse forced another fresh spoonful into my mouth, as well as some that I had regurgitated. This despicable act was repeated over and over, until I had "eaten" all of the Spanish rice.

Looking back on it now, I'm sure if I had choked to death, the hospital would have defended the nurse by claiming it was an accident. And I'm also certain that's why I had the reaction I did, back in high school, when I, once again, encountered this detestable concoction.

I had just received my tray of food from the serving counter in the cafeteria, and walked over to the table my friends were occupying. After sitting down with them, I picked up my fork and was just about to begin eating, when I saw it on my plate. I'm sure the guys thought I had gone completely "wacko" when I just sat there staring at it, as those old memories began flooding my mind. Then, without any explanation, I picked the tray back up and began walking defiantly toward the waste disposal area. But instead of sitting it down on the counter inside the window, I threw it as hard as I could toward the garbage container, then promptly left the building.

I apologize for regressing from my original story, but maybe now I can finally lay that old memory to rest. Uhm, "journal therapy" you reckon?

Anyway, once the nurse was satisfied enough of the Spanish rice was gone from my plate, she proceeded to jerk me by the arm to my bed...then, unceremoniously, put me in it. Needless to say, that turned out to be another evening I wasn't allowed to watch TV. So I just lay there thinking of Mom and Dad and wishing I were back home, until finally crying myself to sleep.

My Ordeal

I didn't think that first Sunday was ever going to come. And I wasn't quite prepared for my reaction when it did. As soon as visitors began trickling in around two, I stood in my bed and began watching the big double doors, waiting for my parents to walk through them. Inexplicably, when they did, I immediately began to cry. And my tears came even harder when Mom threw her arms around me and gave me that much longed-for kiss and hug. I'm sure Dad thought I was a big baby, as he proceeded to pat me on the back. But he didn't know what all I'd gone through during the long, horrible week that had just passed.

However, my tears quickly began to dry when Mom pulled a box of candy from the paper bag she was carrying. And how could they not have? Coconut bonbons with a chocolate covering! My "favoritist" thing in the whole world! But wouldn't you know it, when a nurse saw Mom open the box, she walked over and asked her to only let me have one piece, since our evening meal would be served immediately after visiting hours ended.

After the nurse placed the box of candy in my side of the cabinet, I began filling my parents in on all the grizzly details of what had transpired during my "internment" at the hospital. After finishing, I jammed the last bite of candy into my mouth, then waited for their reaction. But when they just looked at one another and smiled, I realized it was hopeless. They thought I was just making up stuff, so they would get me out of there. That's when it finally dawned on me, that if I were ever going to get "busted" out of that place, it would be by my own devices.

When visiting hours were over, I tried desperately to hold back the tears I felt rushing straight to my eyeballs, but that was just as hopeless. They came even harder than before! Especially, when I had to watch as my parents walked back through those big doors, leaving me there to "rot in my cell."

However, I do think I slept a little better that night, than any of the others since being detained in that terrible place. Just seeing my parents again was a big relief. And although my stories weren't believed, just being able to get them off my chest helped a lot, too.

The next morning, I awoke to a strange, moaning sound, coming from somewhere nearby. Rubbing my eyes to make sure I wasn't dreaming, I raised up in my bed to see what it was. When I did, I noticed the oddest sight. The little boy in the bed next to mine was lying on his side, clutching his tummy. But what was even odder, his mouth and most of the area around it were coated with a brown substance.

I just sat there for several seconds, observing his weird behavior. But when my nose caught the distinct smell of chocolate and coconut, I immediately swung over the top of my bed railing, dropped to the floor, and began crawling to the cabinet. Upon reaching it, I yanked the door open, only to see an empty box staring back at me. The little future "porch pirate" had snuck into my side of the cabinet and made off with my candy!

A nurse, who happened to be walking by, noticed what was going on, and rushed over to put me back in my bed. She then went hurrying off, and returned a few minutes later with a doctor. Confused at what had taken place, he went straight to work examining the little boy. However, it didn't take a brain surgeon to diagnose what his problem was. In fact, I could've done it myself, and saved the doctor a lot of time. But, fortunately, the nurse alertly noticed the open cabinet door, as well as the empty candy box, then stood and turned to me.

"Did you eat all of that candy? She asked.

I just gave her a scowl while passively pointing to the little boy, and replied, "I wish I had!"

That drew a big chuckle from the doctor, who then turned and whispered something to the nurse. However, I failed to see the least bit of humor in the situation. Thoroughly miffed, I just slumped back against my pillow, crossed my arms and watched as both the doctor and nurse left the kid's bedside. But it wasn't long until I had something to laugh about, too.

The nurse quickly returned, along with another one who was holding a bottle in her hand. They then proceeded to restrain the little boy, while forcing him to open his mouth. When he was no longer able to struggle, one of the nurses delivered two heaping table spoons of castor oil into it. What followed was priceless! Well, at least for me, it was. As soon as he was released, the little "rug rat" came up spitting and gagging, with an expression on his face resembling that of a possum who had chomped down on a green persimmon.

I couldn't help but laugh at justice being served, and even though I was holding my hand over my mouth, one of the nurses noticed.

"Do you want some of this, too?" she flippantly asked while waving the bottle in front of my face.

Naturally, I had to graciously decline her generous offer... then quickly rolled over and pulled the covers over my head.

Unfortunately, I do have to admit that the candy-pilfering little boy did manage to get the last laugh, though. That evening, as he and I were taking our baths together, the warm, soapy water aided the greasy laxative in achieving its desired result. I suddenly heard a loud gurgle and blurp come from deep in the tub, only to look down and see my bonbons come bobbing to the surface.

And I must also admit, not all of my experiences at the hospital were as unpleasant as the ones I've heretofore described. One in particular took place about half way into my stay there. I remember a nurse bringing me a rather colorful pair of shorts, and telling me to put them on. Confused, but not about to ask any more questions, I removed my pajamas and pulled the weird garment up around my waist...as did all the other boys. While we were doing this, she proceeded to inform us that we were going to the indoor pool for a swim.

I had absolutely no idea what a pool was, other than the mud holes in our driveway that Mamma tried to keep me out of. But I certainly didn't think she'd be referring to anything like that. However, I sure knew what swimming was...although I couldn't do it...which just happened to be my other "favoritist" thing in the whole world!

There were two little creeks near our house. One of them was Muddy Creek, a meandering little stream about a mile south of where we lived, which provided a section of the southwestern border between Burke and McDowell Counties. And which, by the way, always seemed to live up to its name. The other, Silver Creek, an equal distance to the north, contrarily, had never lived up to its name, as it had been a source of gold extraction during the early nineteenth century.

I think the latter was my favorite because of a swimming hole located on it, referred to as the Mill Shoals by the locals. This was a stretch of swift water flowing over some long, flat rocks. The rocks had been worn smooth by the many swimmers who had been sliding down them for decades. They led to a large pool at the bottom, where an old grist mill once stood. However, if that's what the nurse meant by a pool, I could never imagine getting anything like that inside a building!

Suddenly, a long line of wheelchairs came rolling into the room, pushed by, what looked to me like, high school age boys and girls. Once all of us kids were helped into them, we were then pushed to a couple of elevators and taken down to the ground floor. A left turn and about fifty feet later, we entered a cavernous room filled with the bluest water I had ever seen! I later learned that this was the aquatic therapy center that us "cripples" were to be turned loose in.

Please excuse my grammar in that last sentence, I was just trying to be "cute." But, anyhoo, for this five year-old boy, who had been confined inside a steel cage for the better part of two weeks, it was sheer heaven!

I couldn't wait to jump in it, and began tugging excitedly on the strap holding me inside the chair, only to receive a slap on my hand and a command to wait my turn. After the two seconds it took me to shake off the humiliating indignation this appalling treatment had caused me, I did just that and waited my turn. And once it came, I was soon splashing around, exuberantly, in the big pool, as though I didn't have a care in the world. However, a short time later, I certainly did! Much too soon, the boys began being taken out and put back in their wheelchairs.

"Are you kidding me? Does somebody have a plane to catch?" I thought to myself.

You've probably figured out by now that I didn't actually think that...but I'm sure it was something pretty similar.

Deeply saddened by what was taking place, and nowhere near ready to come out of the water, I looked around for a place to hide. And what do you know? I just happened to find one!

There were concrete steps leading into the pool, but the sides didn't extend all the way back to the wall. Behind them, was just enough space for me to fit, and still be able to keep my head above water! When I looked around and noticed that no one was watching, I headed straight for them.

"Perfect!" I thought, hunkering down in my little "bunker" to wait for everyone to leave. "Maybe if this polio deal leaves me unable to make an honest living, I'll still be able to pursue a life of crime!" Naw...I didn't think that either.

Then, all of a sudden, whistles started blowing and people began jumping back into the water. Apparently, what had set off this unexpected chain of events, was me overlooking a minor detail in commission of this heinous crime; How was I going to account for that one empty wheelchair?

While I was still squatting down in my once formidable hideout, closely observing the frantic search taking place for the "missing body," a young man finally peered beneath the steps and yelled out, "Here he is!"

Hoping to avoid a messy standoff, I figured it might be best if I just gave myself up, and come out without any gratuitous violence. However, the head nurse didn't share my pacifist views, and gave me several hard swats across my backside, before summarily strapping me back inside the wheelchair. Suffice it to say, when we got back to the dormitory, I didn't bother checking out the TV Guide.

When visiting hours finally rolled around after my second week there, I tried my best not to cry when my parents walked into the room. But it was useless. A couple hours a week wasn't nearly enough time for a child my age to spend with his parents. Especially, with so little empathy and kindness being shown by the nurses.

And once again, Mom quickly dried my tears with a loving hug and kiss…and another gift. It wasn't wrapped, just in a paper bag. However, it had the store logo on it, so I knew it had to be something nice! As I was removing it from the bag, I mentioned to them what had become of my candy, the previous Sunday. They both laughed and looked over at the little boy who was being visited by his parents, also.

When I finally had the box out and lying on my lap, I couldn't have been more delighted. For it held the neatest little toy train I could imagine! Of course, all I had ever done was imagine, because I'd never actually owned one.

Regardless, the one I now proudly owned was three cars long, and sat atop an approximately twenty-inch square platform made of tin. Centered on the platform was an oval-shaped track with a station and tunnel mounted on opposite sides. A winding stem located on one end tightened a spring inside the base, propelling the little train around the track.

When it was time for my parents to leave, all too soon again, I wasn't quite as sad as I had been the previous Sunday, because I had my train to play with. But to my utter shock and dismay, after only a few minutes of enjoying my new toy, one of the nurses came over and took it away from me. I could only stare in stunned silence as she calmly placed it back inside the box. Then, without any explanation, the nurse unlocked the door I told you about earlier, and took it inside with her. A few seconds later, she came back out of the room and dropped a little plastic horse in my bed. Dumfounded, I could only watch as she casually sauntered back to the nurses' station. But just because I was too "chicken" to say something to her out loud, didn't mean I couldn't *think* of a few choice names to call her…names I'd last heard when Dad hit his thumb with a hammer.

During the two weeks I'd been locked away inside that hospital, I noticed several other children receiving nice gifts from their parents. And like mine, they were taken away, also, and placed inside that mysterious room, never to return. And just as they had done with me, their neat toy was replaced with some cheap, plastic doodad. I knew there was something fishy going on here, and I was determined to get to the bottom of it!

One evening, just a few days later, a nurse approached my bed around nine p.m. I pretended to be asleep, but kept one eye open to make sure she wasn't armed with an extra helping of that vile liquid she'd forced down my throat, a little earlier. However, this time, she walked on past me to the door, then reached into her uniform pocket and removed a key. I kept a close vigil on her as she unlocked the big door and stepped inside the room. Several minutes passed before she reemerged carrying a couple packages in her arms. But this time, instead of stopping to relock the door, she simply kicked it shut with her foot and proceeded to exit the dormitory.

Immediately, my "wheels began turning!" I knew my toy train was probably still being "held hostage" in that room, waiting for me to free it. And why shouldn't I? After all, it was my property and they had no right to take it! So instead of just lying in my bed, brooding over it, as I'd been doing for the past several days, I now had the perfect opportunity to take it back…undo a wrong…let justice prevail…uphold the code of the West! Hi-Ho, Silver!

"Okay, Butch…just calm down a little bit," I told myself. "This is something that needs to be well thought out, with purpose and clarity." Yes, I had quite the vocabulary back then!

After close scrutiny of the big double doors that led into the dormitory, to make sure no one was about to walk through them, I stealthily climbed out of my bed. Well, as stealthily as a five year-old boy with polio can! But I did happen to land a little clumsily, so I looked back again to see if anyone had heard me. When the coast still appeared to be clear, I tippy-toed to the door and cautiously turned the knob. Bingo! It opened right up!

"Hey, maybe I'm cut out for a life of crime, after all!" I "complimented" myself while smiling broadly.

Pulling the door open, I stepped inside then gently closed it behind me. Suddenly, I was engulfed in total pitch black darkness that scared the freaking "bejeebers" out of me! Terrified, I began frantically feeling along the wall for the light switch. After what seemed like an eternity, I finally located it, then flipped it up. When the big, spooky room lit up, I wiped the perspiration from my brow, took a deep breath, then turned to take a look around…and was totally amazed by what I saw.

All four walls were completely covered by shelves, and every single one of them was jam-packed with toys! If Santa Claus had been there with me, he would've had a conniption fit! And why wouldn't he? A huge room filled to the ceiling with toys, and not one child allowed to play with them!

After slowly walking around the room, gazing up at the almost unfathomable display of wonderful treasures, a thought suddenly struck me, "How was I ever going to locate my train among such a preponderance of toys?"

When I finally realized that the only shelves that weren't completely filled, were the ones at the very top, I figured that was probably where it was, since it was one of the last toys taken in there. Did I mention to you that I was a clever little kid?

Now concentrating my search on only the top rows, I began closely surveying the myriad of toys stacked there. Then, just when I was about to give up hope of ever locating my train, something caught my eye. Sitting underneath a much larger one, was a box which looked very similar to the one my mother had given me. Moving closer to get a better look, my face suddenly lit up like a Christmas tree, when I saw a picture of the little train on the side of it.

Patting myself on the back, I just stood there in awe of my awesome awesomeness…until something suddenly dawned on me. How was I going to go about retrieving my toy, being that the top shelves were several feet higher than my reach? Scratching my head, I just happened to look over at one corner of the room, and noticed a large wooden trunk that appeared to be unlocked. Walking over and opening it, I was flabbergasted to find that it was filled to the brim with all of those cheap plastic toys the nurses had been giving us to play with.

Then another thought popped into my head. Maybe I could

move it over to the section of shelves my train was on, then use it to climb to the second shelf. On that shelf, and directly beneath the box containing my train, was another one low enough for me to, also, climb onto...thusly allowing me to gain enough altitude to reach my objective. Did I mention to you that I was a clever little...yeah, I think I did.

However, my little plan turned out to be a lot more difficult than I thought it would. In fact, moving that big, heavy trunk the necessary ten or twelve feet, evolved into quite an undertaking. If I were to rate it in degree of difficulty, I guess it would fall somewhere between constructing the Great Pyramid of Giza, and folding contour bed linen...and in that order! But luckily for me, the tile floor had been waxed recently, so by putting my back to it and pushing hard with my bare feet...although they began spinning in place like a guinea pig on a treadmill...I somehow managed to maneuver the unwieldy, wooden vessel beneath my toy train.

When that ten-minute ordeal was finally over, I just slumped down on the toy chest like an elephant hunter would sit atop his downed tusker. I needed a little time to catch my breath and tenderly rub the soles of my still burning feet, while contemplating the sound reasoning behind nailing metal shoes to mules' hooves.

If during the course of reading this book, I sometimes seem to be a little too descriptive, or go into too much detail while depicting many of these events, there's something I probably need to point out to you. My publisher advised me that I should try to get this book to around 200 pages, if possible.

Anyhow, with no time to waste, I very quickly got busy again with the task at hand. After climbing onto the big wooden trunk, I then used it as a stable launching platform to scale past the second shelf, and eventually gain a precarious toehold on the third.

With this accomplished, I grabbed hold of the shelf my train was sitting on with my left hand, then gingerly reached for the train box with my right. But wouldn't you know it, when I began tugging on it, the dang box wouldn't budge!

"Well, it looks like that's the end of this little caper," I thought. "I guess some things are just beyond the capability of a scrawny, little, polio-ridden, country hick."

Did any of you actually believe I thought that? If so, you've still got a lot to learn about this "honey badger!"

Now, more determined than ever, I let go of the shelf and placed both of my hands on the train box, then gritted my teeth and pulled with all my might…and to my surprise, it finally began to move in my direction!

But, unfortunately, so did everything else on that wall! With a thunderous crash, shelves, toys, boxes, and anything that hadn't been nailed down, came crashing to the floor…and, of course, it all landed directly on top of me. But I had my train!

Or did it have me? Even though the heavy, wooden chest had caught the even heavier shelves before they could reach me, I was, nevertheless, pinned helplessly beneath the debris. As I lay there clutching my toy train, one tiny glimmer of hope slightly brightened the dark despair engulfing my mind.

"Maybe no one had heard it!" I tried to convince myself. "Yeah, right."

Suddenly, I heard the door open, followed by a loud, bloodcurdling scream. The next thing I knew, nurses came running into the room and began frantically "digging" me out from beneath the rubble. When all of the toys had finally been moved, someone reached for the one in my hands…but I wouldn't let go. I had almost died for that toy train, and the only way they were going to take it from me, was to pry it from my cold, dead fingers!

Yeah, I know. I probably got too caught up in the moment, and over reacted just a teeny, tiny bit when this happened. But there's one other thing I probably need to point out. I was quite the "drama queen" back then. But I was also very pragmatic, and knew when to give up.

So, hopelessly outnumbered, I reluctantly allowed the nurse to take my train, and was then "perp walked" back to my "cell," while holding my hands high above my head. Then, following several punitive smacks to my vulnerable backside, a doctor was called to my bed. Upon arriving, he proceeded to examine me for any possible injuries I may have sustained in the fall…while laughing out loud the whole time.

He eventually gave me a clean bill of health, then placed me back into the custody of the less jovial nurses. I started to ask one of them if my TV privileges were going to be suspended again for the following evening, then figured it might be a little more prudent…if I just kept my big "trap" shut.

While lying in my bed, seriously contemplating what had just transpired, several thoughts entered my mind. I knew the nurses were wrong to take my train, and I also knew I was right in trying to take it back. But, apparently, "right" doesn't always win. So I thought I'd just file the little episode away as a very valuable lesson, learned in my very tender years. Then, at least, I'd be able to walk away from this disaster with a much clearer understanding of the "real" world, as well as witnessing a very poignant and important demonstration...that life ain't always like the movies.

A couple weeks after this now laughable incident had taken place, I experienced an event that wasn't quite as funny. And I'm certain it had a very profound effect on my emotional wellbeing, as well as my future psychological development. Even today, I still have nightmares regarding it, in some form or other.

It all began one evening as we were preparing for our daily TV viewing...well, the other kid's TV viewing, as I was still banned from this particular activity. One of the nurses walked into the ward and made a rather startling announcement. She informed us that instead of our normal evening routine, we would be going to the auditorium to see a show featuring Fred Kirby, a well-known children's entertainer on Charlotte's WBTV.

The nurse went on to say that Mr. Kirby was a cowboy impersonator, and would be playing his guitar and singing children's songs. When she finished, I meekly raised my hand, but before I could say anything, the nurse just smiled and said, "Yeah...you, too."

Even though I had no idea who Fred Kirby was, since we didn't own a television, I still breathed a big sigh of relief...because I sure didn't want to be left alone in that creepy place.

But he was a cowboy, and that's all I needed to know...although I still had no clue what "impersonator" meant, and couldn't figure out the "auditorium" deal, either. However, none of that stuff mattered, because whatever it was, it sure beat the heck out of "festering" away, all by myself, in that dark and drab dungeon they called a dormitory, with nothing to occupy myself with, but a stinking plastic horse!

Suddenly, a long line of wheelchairs came rolling...I think we're all familiar with the procedure, by now. Once all of us boys were loaded into them, the nurses and crew began pushing us toward the elevators. However, this time, when we reached the ground floor, they proceeded in the opposite direction of the pool. Then, just a short distance down the wide hallway, we entered another dormitory very similar to ours, except that it was bigger…much bigger.

But that wasn't all. Inside the darkened room was row after row of some type of weird machines, which resembled large barrels laying on their sides, atop stands with wheels attached to them… and they were all making loud, breathing sounds. However, that wasn't what was scaring the ebee geebees out of me. For protruding from these machines, on the ends nearest the narrow aisle we were being rolled down, were people's heads.

Recoiling with fright, I just watched as about a dozen nurses tended and talked to the poor patients inside those machines. It seemed to take forever to reach the big double doors at the other end of the room. But when we did, I finally exhaled, then asked the nurse pushing my chair what it was that we just passed through. She matter-of-factly explained to me that the people were inside respirators, or "iron lungs," to aid them in breathing. She also went on to inform me that the patients had the same type of polio I had, but much more severe. At hearing this, what little confidence and courage I had remaining, suddenly flew back home without me. And I couldn't help but think that the nurse had provided me with just a little more information than she needed to.

With my brain still occupied with what I had just witnessed, we soon exited the lobby at the end of the respirator room, and entered the auditorium. The nurses proceeded to push us down the aisle, to an area in front of the first row of seats. Thankfully, those terrible thoughts were quickly pushed from my mind when a "cowboy" suddenly appeared from behind the stage curtain!

He was dressed in full western regalia, sporting a pair of ivory-handled six-shooters, resting in black leather, silver concho-laden holsters, which were buckled loosely around his waist. Remember what I told y'all earlier about being overly descriptive? Good!

After singing a song, accompanied by the guitar he was carrying, Mr. Kirby proceeded to tell us cowboy stories, followed by more songs. Soon, all my worries and concerns just drifted away, and I became lost in the merriment and laughter. But when it all ended, far sooner than I had anticipated, my mind quickly returned to that frightening room. As the nurses began pushing us back out of the auditorium, I hoped that, maybe, they would take an alternate route to the elevators. Did I mention that besides being a clever little kid, I was also overly optimistic?

However, it very soon became apparent to me that we were, again, headed in the direction of the respirator room. So, all I could do was tightly close my eyes, place my hands firmly over my ears, and sink as far down into the wheelchair as possible. Now, I know you're probably thinking that I was being very disrespectful to those patients, and I'm sure you're absolutely right. But none of you had to face the possibility of ending up in one of those terrifying things!

That night I awoke several times, crying from frightening nightmares about being locked inside an iron lung, with no one around to let me out. Little did I know, these dreams would persist for years to come…along with others about nurses stealing my toys, and cramming disgusting things into my mouth, until I was gagging…and various other unimaginable experiences, too horrible to describe.

But there was no one around to soothe my fears, so I just lay there softly crying, while trying to think happy thoughts of home…of Mom coming to my bedside to kiss my cheek, and tell me everything was going to be okay. But she was fifty miles away.

I would like to include an important addendum to the end of this chapter, if I may. Although everything I wrote describing the behavior and conduct of the nurses was true, I did omit a very crucial caveat… and I omitted it at the time, simply for the sake of dramatic effect.

What I failed to explain…and in my defense, didn't learn about until doing further research during my second writing of this book… was the almost unbelievable stress those nurses were under.

When the polio epidemic broke out in the region in 1948, and again in 1952, mostly among children, the Asheville Orthopedic Hospital became the only facility in western North Carolina that would accept these patients. Soon, there were approximately 15 new cases being admitted every day, with the nurses struggling to adjust to the new treatment regimen. The hospital reached its peak of 300 patients shortly before I got there, and new wings and additions had to be added on. When the existing staff ultimately became overwhelmed, the hospital called in 100 additional nurses from the Red Cross. To make a bad situation even worse for the overworked nurses, they were forced to live in tents and sleep in cots supplied by the army.

Also keep in mind, these brave nurses didn't have to be there, treating patients suffering from a terrible disease for which there was no prevention or cure…then enduring the added humiliation of people shunning them in restaurants and on buses, when learning they had come from the hospital. So when I "bellyached" and threw my little temper tantrums over the treatment I received from them, just consider that, maybe, there might have been very good reasons why some of them didn't come across as "Miss McGillicuddy."

No Place Like Home

If my memory serves me correctly, I believe the total amount of time I remained "incarcerated" at the Asheville Orthopedic Hospital was approximately six weeks. So you can pretty well imagine how excited I was when I finally got the news, on a Friday morning, that I would be going home the following Sunday. I think I immediately climbed out of bed, jerked my cabinet door open and began throwing all of my things into an empty pillow case!

While I may be exaggerating just a little, I'm almost certain the first words that came out of my mouth after getting the welcome news was, "What time, Sunday?" Because I distinctly remember a nurse telling me that my parents would be there around nine a.m. to get me.

"Great galloping horny toads!" was all I could think to say in reply, because I was beginning to believe I might never see my home again…and it may even have been a figment of my imagination. But if what the nurse had told me was true, this Sunday, I would be leaving the hospital *with* my parents, instead of, sadly, watching them walk back through those big swinging doors without me.

I had really missed my brother and sister, because children under the age of twelve weren't allowed to enter the hospital… unless, of course, they had polio like me. And I also missed playing with my cousins and neighborhood friends. But more than anything else, I missed going to sleep at night in my very own bed, with the added security of knowing my mom and dad were in the very next room. As all of these thoughts continued running through my head, it was all but impossible for me to sleep that night, but somehow I managed.

Surprisingly, when I awoke the next morning, there was a flurry of activity taking place in the dormitory. Nurses had begun pushing carts loaded with boxes into the room, and placing them, individually, on top of our cabinets. While this was going on, we were taken from our beds for breakfast. But I'm sure most of us kids were busier gawking at the strange goings-on than eating… at least, I know I was.

When breakfast was over and we were placed back in our beds, doctors came into the dorm and, with the assistance of the nurses, began removing strange objects from the boxes. But oddly enough, there hadn't been a box placed next to my bed.

From what I could deduct, with my limited knowledge of the situation at the time, it appeared the doctors and nurses were giving the boys some kind of neat toy. They appeared to be shoes with a metal device extending from them. When a nurse finally walked by my bed, I asked her if I was going to be getting one. She just smiled and shook her head, "No."

"Worked over, again!" I thought, throwing myself back down into my bed and crossing my arms. "What's a little kid got to do to get ahead around here?"

And it sure didn't do anything to get them off my "bad side" when the boys were taken from their beds and helped to walk around, with those "toys" attached to their legs.

However, when a doctor, accompanied by a nurse, walked over to my bed, it appeared as though things may finally be looking up. The nurse proceeded to remove my pajamas so the doctor could thoroughly look me over, including all four limbs. But when he had finished, the doctor just smiled, patted me on the head and said to the nurse, "Looks like we have a lucky one here!" Then, the nurse put my pajamas back on and they proceeded to walk to another bed.

"Yeah, right! I've been nothing but "lucky" ever since I was thrown into this dump," was all I could think. However, later on, I realized just how lucky I was!

The boys, of course, were being fitted with braces on their legs, which had suffered muscle atrophy because of the polio. With some of them, it only involved one leg...but with others, it was both. And one kid was particularly unlucky, as all four of his limbs had been afflicted. Looking back on it now, I feel so ashamed of my indifference and ignorance of their horrific ordeal...as well as guilt that I was, somehow, able to escape that same terrible fate.

I don't think I slept a wink that night, and was standing in my bed, anxiously waiting, when the nurses came around at seven to remove us for breakfast. When I was placed back in it, thirty minutes later, I pointed to the big clock on the wall and asked the nurse where the nine was. She just laughed and pointed it out to me. However, I failed to see any humor in my request, and to show my displeasure, gave her a cold, hard stare as she turned to leave. I then began closely monitoring the clock, but noticed there were three hands on the dang thing, and had no idea which one of them would tell me when it was nine o'clock.

So I started out watching the long, skinny one, because it was moving a lot faster than the other two. But every time it got to the nine, and I looked over at the big double doors leading into the dormitory, wouldn't you know it…nothing happened. Undeterred, I decided to keep my eye on the thicker long one, instead. But, unfortunately, I got the same result when it finally reached the nine, a short while later. Totally confused and frustrated, I just threw myself back down in bed, because I sure as heck wasn't about to watch the short one. That little sucker barely budged! Then, suddenly, I had a fantastic idea and stood back up.

"I know," I thought to myself. "I'll just stand here and watch those big doors, instead of that stupid clock! That's where my parents will be entering the room, anyway. So, if I just stand here and watch 'em, it'll make the time pass a lot faster. So, that's what I'll do…and no one had better try to stop me. I'm just gonna stand…right here…watching…those…doors…until………

Suddenly, I felt a hand shaking me, so I just rolled over and pulled the covers above my head, while thinking, "Gee whiz, can't a little kid get any sleep around this place?"

Then, I heard a woman's voice that sounded vaguely familiar saying, "Hey, I thought someone was just raring to go home?"

BAM!!! Like a rocket, I sprang to my feet and threw my arms around my mother.

However, my excitement was tempered, somewhat, when Dad just patted me on the head and dryly commented, "I don't know what your big hurry is. It looks to me like you've got it made here."

With my arms still locked tightly around Mom, I just stared coldly at him, as a thought popped into my head, "You know, if that guy wasn't my dad, I'd probably slap the slobber out of his mouth!"

But fortunately for him, my resentment at his feeble attempt at humor was quickly swept aside when Mom just laughed and handed me a big brown paper bag containing my street clothes. When I looked inside and saw them, I couldn't get out of my pajamas fast enough!

"Whoa...slow down a little! You're gonna rip the buttons plum off of those things!" my mother scolded, when I began tearing at them like a starving monkey peeling open a ripe banana.

Shaking her head at my complete lack of patience, Mom began helping me out of my pajamas and into my outdoor togs. As soon as this was done, I stood up in bed and shouted, "Let's go!"

"Not so fast, young'un," Mom said. "You're letting the 'tail get a little ahead of the cat.' We have to wait for the doctor to come around and officially release you."

Not wanting to hear that, I just slumped against the bed railing, while letting go a deep sigh. But then I figured I'd already spent half of my life in that place, so what's a few more minutes going to hurt?

When a doctor finally arrived at my bedside, he began discussing my condition with my parents. He explained to them that I had contracted respiratory polio, the strain that afflicts the body's upper torso region. He went on to say that my legs and arms weren't affected, and I shouldn't have any future problems with them. However, there was a very good chance that my affected back and chest muscles could further deteriorate, causing my rib cage to collapse onto my already weakened diaphragm. He went on to say that if this were to happen, I would have to wear a back brace. And the condition could possibly become so severe that it would be difficult or impossible for me to breathe. In this case, the only remedy would be an iron lung.

I guess it was a darn good thing I didn't understand half the words the doctor was saying, and my already short attention span was well on its way back home. Otherwise, I'm sure I would've had a much different reaction than the "ho-hum" attitude I displayed.

However, I did get a little hint that everything wasn't going to be as "honky-dory" as I thought it might, when my mom began to cry…although she did try hard to conceal it…and Dad just took a deep breath and looked down at the floor.

Of course, the doctor anticipated the despondent reaction his dire prognosis would cause my parents, and promptly added, "Now, what I just gave you was a worse-case scenario. If a strict exercise regimen is put in place as soon a possible, then, over time, these muscles could be strengthened enough that the major problems I just mentioned could be avoided. However, it won't be easy, and will require a lot of hard work…on everyone's part."

I could tell that second, less glum diagnosis, provided by the doctor, seemed to have relieved my mother somewhat, as she released a deep sign and began patting me on the back. As for my father, though, he was a little harder to read. But that clinched jaw and fierce look of determination didn't bode well for me… and just a couple weeks later, I would know exactly what it meant.

Still yet, none of that seemed to be registering all that high on my "concern meter," as my only thought was getting out of that place and going home. However, there did happen to be a completely unrelated matter that I was plenty concerned about!

When we were finally ready to leave, I looked up at Mom and motioned with my finger for her to lean down. When she did, I whispered into her ear something about the whereabouts and accessibility of a certain toy train. No...I didn't use those exact words, but you readers should be able to put yourselves in the place of a five-year old kid, and figure it out.

Mama just nodded, then walked over to where a nurse was seated at a desk. After a short conversation, I detected an expression on my mother's face that began causing me even more concern. After walking back to my wheelchair, she leaned over again and informed me that the nurse had requested that we donate the train to needy children. From the look on her face, I could tell Mom thought that that would be the "Christian" thing to do, and I would get nowhere in protesting her decision.

However, that didn't prevent a grimace from forming on *my face* when I mulled her decision around in my brain for a few seconds, before asking the inevitable question. One that I prudently muttered in a barely audible whisper, because it contained a couple words I had learned from my father. "Dad-burn it, (not the word) who in the heck (not the word, either) could be needier than me?"

Fortunately, by that time, my "better angels" had finally taken control of my emotions, and the answer to my question became clear as day!

"Heck, if my train being held for ransom, is the price I have to pay to be released from this old "hoosegow," then I don't reckon I should complain?" I reasoned. Some of you younger readers may have to google the word in quotation marks.

When the wheelchair I was sitting in, was pushed by a nurse through the exit on the ground floor, with my parents following along behind, I felt like jumping out and kissing the ground! If I could've only seen the ground....or anything, for that matter! It seems my eyes had become unaccustomed to the sunlight, and everything was just a giant, bright blur to me.

But when I was finally able to see again, I couldn't help but stare at the beautiful trees, the beautiful mountains, the beautiful clouds, the beautiful fire hydrants, the beautiful manhole covers...you get the picture. However, nothing looked more beautiful to me than Dad's old dilapidated, rundown '46 Chevrolet Stylemaster!

I'm sure my parents noticed the new "giddy-up" in my step when I suddenly helped myself from the wheelchair and began making a "beeline" for the old car. Words can't begin to describe my relief when the three of us were finally in it, and Dad pulled out of the parking lot and onto the hospital drive...this time, in a much more favorable direction.

However, for some macabre reason, I just had to turn around in my seat for one final look back. I wasn't able to see the building when I was first brought there, so I didn't want all of my memories of the place to be of the inside, only. But when I did, I immediately regretted the decision!

Although it was a relatively new building, erected in the late 1930's, I was shocked by its gothic, European appearance. Built entirely of drab, gray stone, with a wing extending from each side, the two story building was made to appear even more sinister by the rather large portico at the front entrance and the three creepy dormers that had been added to the roof.

Quickly turning back around in my seat, I tried hard to get that picture out of my mind. And in the process, the words to that old Negro spiritual began echoing in my head; "Free at last, free at last! Thank God Almighty, I'm free…" Okay, that didn't really happen, either…so I'm not about to take credit for it. However, years later, when I heard those same words reverberating from our television, you can bet the ranch that I knew exactly how the great man felt!

There was no interstate highway system back then, so the fifty-mile drive home seemed to take forever. And it was no wonder, as we were forced to follow the little two-lane highway down the mountain and through the middle of every "one-horse" town along the way…kind of like driving through Canada, today! Nevertheless, I knew I was finally home when that big, white-frame farmhouse suddenly came into view!

Home Where I Grew Up

Asheville Orthopedic Hospital-circa early 1950's

Me Shortly Before Contracting Polio

Crawley Family- Christmas 1957 I'm at bottom left "cowboying up"

A Young Boy's Plight

As good as it felt to be back home again, I could immediately tell things weren't going to be quite the same as before. I got this impression when Dad sat me down and went over all of the things the doctors had discussed with my mother and him at the hospital.

He said they were told that I would be weak for an unknown period of time, depending on how quickly I regained some of my strength, because of the damage done to my back and chest muscles. My father also told me I would experience difficulty breathing, when running and playing, because of my weakened diaphragm. So I would need to rest for a while, before getting back to my normal routine.

Aw, dang it! Who am I trying to kid? My dad would never say anything like that! That sounds more like something Ozzie Nelson would say to Ricky…not anything remotely close to what my old man would tell me! It was more like, "You've got one more week of living the "good life," because that's what the doctors told us to do. Then, the "mollycoddling" will be over with! You hear me, boy?"

Still yet, none of that was what made the hairs on the back of my neck stand up...but what he included with it, did. He also informed me that the doctor said that I shouldn't be treated any differently than my two siblings. In fact, he and Mom might need to be a little tougher on me, so I wouldn't get used to being pampered. But you know what? I always suspected he pulled that last bit of advice from somewhere down around his gluteus maximus. Because that's exactly how I was treated *before* I got sick! And wouldn't you know it, it was only a few hours later when I got first-hand experience with this new and improved, "tough on Butch" approach to child rearing.

It seems Johnsie and Ozelle had come over to welcome me back home, and see how I was doing. They were sitting at the foot of my bed, catching me up on all the "comings and goings" in the neighborhood since I'd been away. Suddenly, Dad appeared at the door and told them I wasn't allowed company. I guess he thought they may have been pampering me just a little too much.

And just a couple weeks into this "no-coddle" experiment, things got worse...a lot worse. Dad had just arrived home from work one morning, and ordered me out of bed. He then told me to get dressed and meet him in our back yard. Still groggy from just waking up, I was standing there rubbing my eyes and yawning when he walked out the back door. Little did I know that I was in for a literally rude awakening, as Dad began putting the doctor's solid advice and my frail body to the test.

I still didn't know what to make of it when he removed his shirt and began demonstrating the proper way to do jumping jacks, then had me join in. But when he suddenly began bellowing out, "hup-two-three-four" at the top of his lungs, I just knew he'd lost it!

After doing the jumping jacks until it felt as though my lungs were about to quit on me, and I was going to collapse to the ground, he suddenly yelled, "Fall out!"

I just looked at him with a bewildered expression, and between huffs, sarcastically asked, "Fall out of what?"

Dad, apparently not appreciative of my sense of humor, then shouted, "Just sit the hell down!"

I quickly dropped to the ground, then looked up at the kitchen window where I knew Mom was busy preparing breakfast. Suddenly, I remembered a story she had told us kids a few months earlier. It was a funny tale about how she had met my father, a short time after he returned from the war. She said they were walking hand-in-hand down the old dirt road her family lived on when a plane flew by, right overtop their heads. To her astonishment, Dad immediately pulled her over into the ditch and then fell on top of her. At first, she thought he was just being overly romantic, until she noticed the frightened look on his face, and realized he was having flashbacks from his combat experiences.

I wanted so badly to yell to Mom, "They're baaaaack!" But I knew that wouldn't be a good idea.

My air intake had just about caught up with the amount my body had consumed, when I heard Dad yell, "Back up!"

Struggling to get upright and back on my feet, I began thinking that if I just humored him, this would eventually wear off and he'd lose interest. Just like the time he bought that old used guitar, and thought that, in no time at all, he'd be playing it just like his hero and look-a-like, Ernest Tubb. For months, he listened to our old radio, blasting out every song the "Old Troubadour" sang, while trying his best to play and sing along.

"Gosh, I sure hope this doesn't turn into something that awful!" I thought.

When Dad suddenly shouted, "On the ground!" then dropped flat on his stomach, I was starting to think he'd really come "unglued."

Scratching my head, I looked down at him and meekly asked, "I thought you just said to get up?"

"Don't get smart with me, boy!" was all it took for me to drop to the ground like a rock!

After he was satisfied I was in the proper position, Dad expertly demonstrated the proper form and technique required for doing push-ups. When this was accomplished, the "hup-two-three-four's" began again, signaling me to join the "fun!" As I began straining to push my severely weakened chest up off the ground with my two aching arms, I found myself having a few "flash-backs" of my own, "You know, maybe that hospital wasn't so bad, after all!"

The whole time I was struggling to do the push-ups, Dad stood over me yelling and prodding me on. When I just couldn't do anymore of them, he finally relented and ordered me to stand. Slowing getting to my feet, while gasping for air, Dad then began instructing me in a drill he called "deep-breathing exercises." This consisted of me taking a deep breath and holding it, while he ran off a count of, "one thousand and one, one thousand and two" and so on, until I was forced to exhale. I think I only made it to the count of ten that first time. But even then, my lungs felt like they were going to burst out of my chest. But Dad, being the brutal taskmaster he was, made me continue until I could make it to twenty.

After that was concluded, I was familiarized with a regimen where I stood with both hands on my hips. Then, at the cadence, I would extend my arms straight out…then bring my hands back to my waist…then straight up…then back to my shoulders, where the routine would start over, all at a very rapid pace. Try this for ten minutes and see where your heart rate goes!

We then finished the session with set-ups, which I think are self-explanatory, and all of you readers, I'm sure, are familiar with. When I could no long raise my exhausted torso up off the ground, Dad finally showed a little compassion and yelled, "Fall out!" And boy, did I! He then allowed me to go back inside, where I received a pitiful stare from Mom, and instructions to go cleanup for breakfast.

Later on, my dad put a chin-up bar in the willow tree, which I spent many "wonderful" hours hanging on to. This was soon followed by a weight bench he cobbled together from some old left-over lumber…and a bench-press bar, fashioned from a forty-inch long steel pipe, with six, eight-pound window weights attached to the ends with bailing wire. Don't you just love his ingenuity?

You know, deep inside, I'm sure I appreciated the motive behind all the trouble and effort my father was going through, to prevent the dire prognosis of the doctors from becoming a reality. But I couldn't help but think that he may be enjoying it just a little too much. So with this daily routine sapping me of my physical strength, along with the possibility of having to wear a back brace…or heaven forbid, being stuck in an iron lung for the rest of my life…robbing me of my mental well-being, I began sinking into a deep, dark state of depression.

Now you know why I made the statement earlier, about dreading the sound of Dad's car pulling into the driveway every morning. And every night, I would pray to God that he would, somehow, deliver me from this sad plight, then cry myself to sleep because my prayers continued to go unanswered…until I found that beautiful Collie pup!

The Second Coming

Or was it Shep who had found me? After all, there were four other houses between ours and the Haskins residence, and he could've easily gone in the opposite direction. But what would lead an eight week-old pup to leave a home where he was loved and taken care of, in the first place? And I know he was loved! I could tell that by the way the Haskins sisters reacted when they found him in our front yard.

But even if he had simply decided to run away, what would've led him to my house...then, just lay down next to the chimney, as if he were waiting there for me to find him? It just didn't add up…didn't make any sense, at all!

It had been about a week since Betty and Mule had come to get Shep…just couldn't bring myself to think of him as Jimmy… and all that time, I was unable to get him off my mind. At least two or three times a day, I would walk down to the end of our driveway and just stare up the road at the Haskins house. While doing so, I couldn't help but wonder what he was doing, how he was being kept, were they being kind to him. But most of all, was he missing me as much as I was missing him?

On one such occasion, Mom came walking down to where I was seated, worried that I was too close to the road for my safety. After instructing me to move back a short distance, she turned and started back to the house. But after taking only a few paces in that direction, Mom suddenly wheeled around and began walking slowly back towards me…then just stood there, silently, for a few seconds, expressing a look of total frustration.

"Butch, you're gonna worry yourself to death over that pup!" she finally said. "If God means for you to have him, then I believe you will. But sitting here feeling sorry for yourself ain't helping anything. You're just gonna have to try to get on with your life, and leave all of this in God's hands. He'll always do what's best for you."

"Well, he sure as heck has, so far," was my only thought…one I made sure I kept to myself. But I knew Mom meant well…and that's just the way she was. My mother seemed to always possess a deep, abiding faith that everything was, ultimately, in God's hands, and we were eventually steered in the direction he intended us to go…*if* we prayed hard enough, and had faith in his plan.

When she turned again to walk away, I just looked dejectedly down at the ground. Then, in a fit of anger, I jerked up a handful of grass and flung it defiantly toward the road, while letting loose a "cuss" word. Of course, I made sure Mom was no longer watching me before doing all that. Then, just as quickly, I began thinking about what she had just said to me, and immediately felt ashamed.

"Why not?" I thought. "I've tried everything else."

So this time, I approached my problem with just a little more reverence and piousness. Gazing heavenward, I whispered a short, but solemn, prayer. It was the only one I knew besides the dinky, little bedtime "ramble" we were taught…or the dry, standard blessing we were made to recite at mealtime. This was one I occasionally heard my mother whisper, almost under her breath, when a problem became too much for her to deal with, or when she wasn't quite sure of the course she should take.

"Not my will, but thine be done," I humbly beseeched, while wiping away a tear that had found its way onto my cheek. Then rising to my feet, I took one final, doleful glance in the direction of the Haskins house. And when I did, I almost had to rub my eyes in disbelief. For running down the road toward me, as fast as his little legs could "churn", was Shep!

I dropped to my knees just as he barreled into my chest and began affectionately licking my face. As this was taking place, I realized that not only had my prayer been answered, but the burning question I'd asked myself earlier. Yes…Shep had definitely missed me, every bit as much as I had missed him!

After our heart-felt greetings had been exchanged, I stood and began running back to the house, with Shep chasing along at my feet. However, my excitement was dashed somewhat when Mom, who was now sitting in the porch swing, calmly stated, "You do know that you're gonna have to take him back, don't you?"

I just looked down at the pup, who had begun running in circles around my legs, then mournfully back up at Mom, before pleading, "Could I just play with him for an hour, before I do?"

Mom just smiled slightly while nodding her head, then said, "Only for an hour…then I'll go with you to take him back home."

"Home?" I wish she hadn't used that word to identify where Shep had just come from…and where we would soon be returning him. I'm certain he didn't think of it that way. But I couldn't be worrying about anything like that…not now. The only thing that mattered, at the moment, was the one hour I had to spend with Shep. Sixty care-free minutes that wouldn't be spent fixated on my physical problems, and the painful and exhausting exercise regimen that would start my next day. Right now, my only concern was squeezing every second from every minute of my next hour on Earth, until it was permanently seared into my memories. Because, after all, I had no idea if this brief and precious interlude would ever be repeated.

As I ran joyously around our house, with Shep chasing after me while tugging playfully at my frazzled trouser legs, I wished it could be like this forever. That every day would be a repeat of the one that had preceded it…and I would never have to worry about anything, other than how I was going to spend the next one with my new, best friend.

But when I fell exhausted onto the ground, and Shep climbed on my heaving chest and began licking my face, I heard the words I'd been dreading.

"Son, it's time to take him back home," Mom informed me. And yes, she used that infuriating word again.

But without protesting, I scooped Shep up in my arms and began following along behind Mom, as we made our way up the road toward the Haskins house. At first, I didn't say a word. But when Shep realized where he was being taken, and began whimpering, I tried with all my might to think of something…anything…that might prevent what was taking place.

"Mama, is there some way we could buy Shep from the Haskins?" I finally asked.

"Butch, you know your dad wouldn't pay for that pup," she

answered. "Why, he already spends every extra nickel we have on his beagles!"

"I could pick blackberries this summer, and sell them to the neighbors. I know Grandma would buy some…and Joan would probably help me," I desperately pleaded.

"You're way too young to go traipsing off into the woods by yourself," Mom stated. "And besides, we need all the berries we can pick, to get ourselves through the winter. So, just stop it! You knew what had to be done the second that pup ran into the yard."

Fighting back tears, I looked down at Shep, who was looking pitifully up at me, as we turned into the Haskins' driveway. After Mom knocked on the door, it was only a couple seconds until Mrs. Haskins opened it and gave her a warm greeting. When she noticed me holding Shep, she smiled and said, "Oh, you found him! We saw where he had dug out under his fence…and Mule and Betty have been looking for him, all morning!"

Before Mom could respond, Mrs. Haskins turned and yelled back into the house, "Betty, Jimmy's been found!"

"I suspected that's where he was, Mama!" came her reply, just before running out the door and snatching Shep from my arms.

After Mrs. Haskins thanked us and we turned to leave, Mom looked down at me and placed her hand on my shoulder. But then she pivoted back around just before Mrs. Haskins closed the door, and asked, "I don't suppose you'd be interested in selling that pup?"

Immediately, we heard Betty shout from inside the house, "He's not for sale!"

Mrs. Haskins just looked sympathetically at Mom, then down at me, while simply shaking her head.

I didn't wait to walk back with my mother after this sad affair had ended. I just began running as fast as I could back down the road toward the house…then, right on past it and down to the barn. After climbing up in the hay loft, I finally began crying as though my heart had been shattered into a thousand tiny pieces…pieces I had no way of knowing could ever be put back in place.

Fate Unrelenting

In the days that followed, I tried as best I could to put this episode out of my mind. I realized there was nothing more I could do about the sad state of affairs, and any further crying and worrying, on my part, wasn't going to alter it. And although I felt it was only right that Shep remained with me, since it was clearly evident that that's what he wanted, Fate had decided otherwise. I just needed to accept this fact and try to get on with my life. Besides, I had other issues I was currently dealing with that could, potentially, have a greater impact on my wellbeing than a little pup suffering from a bad case of wanderlust...issues which, unless satisfactorily resolved, could adversely affect my life far into the future.

But Fate doesn't always allow us to decide when an important chapter of our lives has been satisfactorily dealt with, and can then be put to rest. It has the power to recognize all consequential obstacles and deterrents that may block or impede our pathway through life, and chart for us a course around them. We're only able to see the things we think are important in the moment. But like some grandmaster chess player, Fate is able to scan the board and determine what move needs to be made in the interim, in order to win the match a dozen moves later.

I now realize this is what was taking place when Dad walked into the kitchen early one morning, after just getting home from work. Although he was whistling, and seemed to be in an unusually good mood, that did little to cheer me up. It had been more than a week since Mom and I had returned Shep to the Haskins, and I'm afraid I was still brooding about it, despite all of my attempts not to.

Joan, Alvin and I were seated along the crude dining table bench Dad had constructed for us, waiting for our mother to serve the hot breakfast she'd just finished preparing. But after seeing my father, my thoughts suddenly shifted to a topic far less appetizing. So, unlike my siblings, whose only concern was the food they were about to eat, I began thinking about what would follow...that dang military basic training workout!

Before taking his usual seat at the head of the table, Dad stopped and whispered something to Mom, who was still standing at the stove. Oddly enough, her only reaction to what he had to say, was just a slow shake of the head, accompanied by a troubled look. After finally sitting down, he took a quick glance over at me, then began filling his plate from the serving bowls Mom had just placed in the middle of the table. While politely waiting my turn, I was also closely observing him from out of the corner of my eye.

Dad had just "speared" a fork full of food and raised it to his mouth when he very strangely paused right there, looked over at me again, and this time asked, "I don't guess you noticed what showed back up on the porch this mornin'?"

Instantly jumping to my feet, I was quickly "reigned" back in by Dad's, "Sit back down, boy! You don't need to be handlin' that old dirty pup, before eatin' your breakfast!"

With my father's admonishment still echoing in my ears, I began filling my plate with food, then cramming it into my mouth with both hands. Although I could tell Mom very much disapproved of my table manners, she didn't say anything. When I had finally gotten it all down, with the exception of one biscuit, I held it up while looking pleadingly at Dad.

"Aw, go ahead," was all it took for me to quickly slide down from the bench, scoot underneath the table, and go scurrying toward the front door, with the biscuit gripped firmly in my hand.

The instant Shep recognized who had run out onto the porch, he sprang up off his mat, and with his tail wagging furiously, scampered over to greet me. I dropped to my knees and wrapped my arms around him, as he began affectionately licking my face. But when he did, I noticed Shep was wearing a collar with a short length of rope tied to it.

Puzzled, I just stared at it as he hungrily gobbled down the biscuit. It was about this time that Dad walked out the front door and stood over us for a few seconds before saying, "Looks like they tried tying him, this time…and he chewed through the rope."

He then squatted down and began untying what was left of it from Shep's collar, while adding, "I imagine the little feller spent the better part of the week gnawin' on it."

"Do we have to take him back, right now?" I asked, almost pleading with my father, while hoping for a favorable response.

Dad thought it over for a few seconds then, surprisingly, gave it.

"Hell no! Let 'em come and git him this time," he stated rather disdainfully. "Anybody that can't keep a little pup from gittin' loose, don't need to own one!"

With a big smile spreading rapidly across my face, I grabbed Shep up in a big hug. However, my new-found good will toward my father turned out to be short-lived, when he abruptly stood and said, "You've got five minutes…then I'll see you 'round back."

Nevertheless, when Dad's "hup-two-three-four's" began reverberating against my eardrums, they weren't met with quite the same contempt as before. I just started doing the jumping jacks, while directing my attention toward Shep. And he simply sat and returned my stare with his little head cocked sideways, as if trying to figure out what type of new game I was playing with him. Then, I guess he decided, "What the heck…a game is a game!" and jumped up and began tugging at my trouser legs, as had always been the routine.

However, "Drill Sergeant" Crawley wasn't about to put up with any shenanigans during one of his workouts, and quickly shouted, "Kick that little mutt the next time he does that…or I will!"

Remembering the fifteen-foot long "lasso" I had braided together using discarded strands of bailing twine, I asked Dad to hold on for just a second. I then went running around to the front porch swing to retrieve it. Upon returning, I looped the noose around Shep's neck, then tied the other end around the willow tree. When this was accomplished, I looked over at Dad for his approval. Apparently satisfied that everything was now in proper order, he once again began his count.

And when he did, the whole routine seemed to go a lot smoother than any of the previous mornings. With Shep curiously looking on, I breezed right through the exercises, without a lot of the pain and exhaustion I had come to expect. Well, to be honest, I'm sure it was still there. I just wasn't paying it as much attention as before. Knowing that my faithful friend was right there beside me, I'm sure, had a lot to do with it.

And upon completion of that morning's workout, I received a welcomed shock! Instead of the "Boy, you're gonna have to do a lot better than that, or we'll be out here the rest of the day!" that I'd normally come to expect, Dad surprisingly closed this session with, "A purty good job! I guess we're done."

After my father had left us and gone back inside the house, I sat down against the willow tree and removed the rope from around Shep's neck. As I affectionately rubbed the furry head he'd placed in my lap, I began planning out our remaining day. And I knew the perfect place to spend it would be the woods below our house. Not only would that familiarize Shep with the portion of our property he'd never been on, but it would also shield him from the Haskins sisters' prying eyes…if, by chance, they happened to walk by our house. Getting to my feet, I began leading my companion in the direction of our barn, and the woods below it. But first, I needed to make sure of the whereabouts of Old Bess.

Old Bess, you ask? Yeah, I suppose I should tell you a little about her. She was our milk cow of pure Guernsey origin…a breed that is known to be docile and unassertive. However, ours was as ornery and belligerent as any bull you'd ever want to meet. And I'm not talking about a Guernsey bull. Oh, no! Bess was more like a Brahman! Anytime she saw someone trespass onto her domain, she'd rush over to make sure they didn't overstay their welcome…which just happened to be the amount of time it took her to get there! Well, except for Dad, whom she had, begrudgingly, extended a "visitor's visa" to. It seems he had "beaned" her over the head with a two-by-four when they were first getting acquainted, which earned him a certain measure of respect…as well as fear.

After locating her way over on the far side of the pasture, where she appeared to be grazing contentedly, I entered the fence through the tight "L" shaped opening, which was too narrow for a cow to maneuver its way through. You could get inside our barn without having to enter the pasture, but I wanted to take Shep around to the other side, where the chicken coop and rabbit pens were located.

Yeah, you heard me right…half-wild rabbits that Dad used for training his beagles. He had started out using fully wild ones that he caught in traps, or rabbit "gums," as we referred to them. However, these rabbits wouldn't survive long enough in captivity to be used for this purpose…and tame rabbits lacked the necessary instincts to evade a pack of pursuing beagles. So, Dad found a source of mixed rabbits that still possessed enough of their wild instincts to outrun a pack of pups, and also be able to survive on their own, after the chase had ended. But the biggest advantage of using these rabbits, was the fact that they could be bred in captivity.

Both the rabbit and chicken enclosures were built onto the back of the barn, next to each other. They were just small, wooden pens nailed together using the same rough, unfinished oak boards the barn had been constructed with. And each had their own six-foot high, chicken wire fence extending out from it. It was my intention to familiarize Shep with these animals, so as to head off any future conflicts which might result.

Yeah, I know you're probably wondering why I would be planning for anything beyond this one day, when the Haskins still legally owned Shep. Well, as I mentioned earlier, I've always been a very optimistic individual, expecting the best while trying not to think about the worst…which for me, back then, was always a lot more likely to happen.

And, unfortunately…or fortunately, depending on one's perspective…I guess I'm still the same today. Like expecting this book to sell several million copies, so I'm finally able to buy that banana plantation and tiki bar in Outer Mongolia someone told me about.

I warned you that I was going to try to work as much humor into this book as possible…even if it's bad. So get used to it!

After leaving the barn, I led Shep to the lower, wooded end of our pasture. There, we slid under the five strands of barb wire and entered my favorite section of the property. This was two acres of thickly-growing yellow pine trees, where us boys would play our "cowboy and Indian" games. My brother, cousins and I, along with some of the neighborhood kids, would build forts and hideouts from pine boughs, in order to fight off Indian attacks. Then, other times, we might be outlaws hiding from the sheriff, after robbing one of the nearby banks.

Inside our pine-bough strongholds, we'd fire our cap guns at the imaginary foes, until the attack was dispatched, or our saddlebags, filled with stolen loot…well, actually, maple and sourwood leaves…were finally secured from the pesky lawmen.

And we'd never pass up a raid when we discovered that Joan, Johnsie and Ozelle had found the sheer brazenness to dare build one of their sissy, little playhouses inside our territory. With guns "blazing," we'd pull apart their puny structures, while riding swiftly by them on our "galloping horses!" And the attacks wouldn't stop until all of the "squatters" and "homesteaders" had been driven out! Gosh, don't that just make you want to be a kid again?

From there, we made our way down to the meandering, little stream, a couple hundred feet below our property line. Growing profusely all along it was a tangled growth of mountain laurel bushes, intermingled throughout with several species of hardwood trees. Suspending from the branches of several of these trees were wild muscadine vines, which we cut off a few feet from the bottom in order to swing from limb to limb through the mountain laurel. This terrific little area was given the name, "the jungle," by us kids, and it's where we played our...well, I'll let you guys try to guess this one.

Okay, Captain Obvious, you made that one a little too easy. But yes, this is where we played our "Tarzan" games, and some of my "favoritest" times were spent there! We kids would swing from tree to tree, pretending to be chased by wild savages, angry gorillas, or some other "peed off" jungle creature, then drop into the refreshing water below when they'd get a little too hot on our trail.

Darn it! I said I wasn't going to do that…but I've done gone and made myself homesick, again!

After leaving there, we spent the rest of the day playing in the vacant field next to the barn. It was covered in broom straw and small field pines, so it made the perfect place to play "hide and seek" with Shep. Mom would send Joan out, occasionally, to check on me. But mostly, she just let me play all I wanted, because both she and Dad knew it was good for my condition.

And Shep was the perfect playmate, running along at my feet with every step I took…then, sitting down next to me whenever I needed to rest. However, all too soon, I heard Mama yelling for me to come inside for supper. As I started walking up the hill toward the house, with Shep running ahead of me, I thought about what an incredible day it had been…something that had become a rarity, since returning home from the hospital.

The good feeling remained with me as I lay in bed that night, with Shep lying on his mat just outside my window. It even carried over into my bed-time prayer. When I finished "blessing" all of my family members, I added a special one for Shep. Then, instead of ending it as I usually did, by asking God to help me overcome my troubling polio symptoms, I requested something different from him. This time, I prayed that if this was too much of a miracle, I would gladly settle for a much smaller one, instead. If he could somehow find a way for Shep and me to remain together, I wouldn't ask for anything beyond that. I would find a way to deal with my problems, without any further complaints or requests.

I know Mom had told me once, that one should never attempt to bargain with God…but I just didn't know any other way to go about it. However, since that time, I've learned that it really doesn't matter how we request things from him, as long as we're sincere and unselfish. But many times we fail to see the beauty, or recognize the genius, in the way our prayers are answered. And I'm certain I failed to see any beauty or genius, a couple weeks later, when Betty showed up in our front yard, carrying a leash.

I was in the backyard playing with Shep, when I overheard Mom talking to someone from our front porch. Finally recognizing Betty's voice, I knelt down next to my friend and gave him a tender hug.

"I guess it's "goodbye" for now, Boy…but we'll be back together again. Just try to stay strong until then…and I will too," I told him.

I then wiped the tears from my eyes and walked around to the front yard. When Betty saw us, she came over and proceeded to snap the leash onto Shep's collar. Then, surprisingly, she looked at me and muttered a quick, but seemingly sincere, "Sorry."

I didn't respond…but, instead, walked over to the porch swing and sat down next to Mom. After patting me on the shoulder, she looked at Betty and said, "I don't want this happening, again, Betty! He's your dog, so it shouldn't be up to us to return him. Whatever you have to do, I don't want him coming back. It's not fair to the boy…and it's not fair to the dog, either!"

Betty, once again, surprised me when she replied, "Ah, I know…and I really don't want him any longer! But Daddy made me come and get him because he was a birthday present…and Daddy's real stubborn. So I guess it's become personal with him now. But anyway, I'll try not to let him get loose again."

As I watched Betty literally dragging Shep down our driveway, I tried with all my might not to cry. But when he turned toward me and began whining, as if to ask, "Why are you letting her do this? I thought we were friends!" It was just too much for me to bear. Suddenly jumping to my feet, I yelled to him as tears began streaming down my face, "Shep, no matter what you have to do…come back to me. I'll be waiting right here!"

Love Triumphant

Even though I was released from the orthopedic hospital in Asheville around mid-September of 1954, that didn't mean I was through dealing with doctors and treatment. I still had to make monthly visits to an outpatient clinic in Morganton, the other small town to the east of us. There, I underwent examinations to determine my current physical condition, and demonstrations as to how I could improve it, along with physical therapy sessions. Although I didn't understand most of the medical terms the doctors used when discussing my prognosis with Dad, I could tell if the news had been good or bad, by his mood on the way home.

And when it proved to be the latter, which always seemed to be the case, it was also reflected in an increase in the severity of my morning workouts. This unrelenting daily routine, coupled with the ever-increasing degree of difficulty the doctors' monthly diagnoses seemed to always precipitate, began taking a tremendous toll on my mind and body.

My mind, I was able to control most of the time, when I

focused my concentration and attention on the more positive aspects of my life...although they seemed to be getting harder and harder to find. However, my body had no way of, likewise, diluting the continuous physical demands being forced upon it. Its only response was to signal to my brain the pain and distress it was being placed under…thusly, creating a vicious cycle of cause and effect.

For some reason, Dad expected me to perform the exercises with the same fervor and gusto he and his fellow army enlistees had displayed during their military training. But they didn't have to suffer with nearly the same degree of pain that I had to, so it wasn't nearly as difficult for them. And because of my extreme youth, I was unable to see anything beneficial resulting from it. So I would usually just go through the motions…and therein lay the seemingly never-ending conflict between my father and me.

Inevitably, my mental well-being began to unravel, as more and more strain was placed on my body. Most nights, my muscles would ache, leading to cramps and muscle spasms, which encumbered my sleep. This, in turn, led to me being lethargic and lackadaisical when aroused from bed for the early morning exercises. Completely unsympathetic to any of this, Dad would only become tougher with me…and he could be a brutal taskmaster when his anger was aroused. In time, I began feeling so bad that I stopped responding to his anger, and that's when things got even worse.

Dad then resorted to a totally different approach. He would remind me of what the doctors had warned us about…the possibility of my chest muscles perishing enough to where I was forced to wear a back brace. And in the rare instances when even that failed to trigger the desired response, he would try to close the deal with the little "thingamajig" about being locked inside an iron lung for the rest of my life…and that always seemed to do the trick!

With hindsight being twenty-twenty, I eventually came to realize what my father was trying to accomplish, as well as the great deal of personal time and effort he was putting into it. I recounted just a couple paragraphs earlier, chapter and verse, the pain and discomfort I had to endure. However, I failed to mention the fact that Dad was suffering from a herniated disc in his upper back, during this same period. This was a very painful condition that, at the time, he didn't know the cause of, and couldn't afford to have surgically corrected, even if he did. Therefore, he received no respite from the immense agony and pain until his late 60's, after decades spent providing for his family.

However, at that juncture in my life, his actions only succeeded in cultivating resentment in me…and laid a foundation of ill-will, which became a very difficult obstacle for me to overcome. Steadily sinking into a tumultuous sea of depression and hopelessness, my life, subsequently, became more and more unbearable, with no relief in sight.

I hope you readers don't mind, but I'm about to take you on a short detour away from the more dour and distressful aspects of my story, because I'm certain it's getting about as difficult for you to read, as it is for me to write. So, if I may, I'd like to share with you a few of the more pleasant moments I experienced during this same time frame. And yes, as hard as it may be for you to believe, I did have some enjoyable moments!

As a matter of fact, one of the first to come to mind took place during one of my workouts. My cousins, Mack and Dean, who lived just up the road from us, dropped by one Saturday morning as they were taking place. The brothers came to the front door, but when they heard the strange sound of Dad's "hup-two-three-four's" emanating from our backyard, they just had to walk around back to check out what was going on.

And when they did, the boys couldn't help but giggle at seeing me doing jumping jacks, with Dad standing in my face barking out the cadence. Now, I shouldn't have to remind you...especially, this far along in the book...that that probably wasn't the best approach for them to take, if they planned on hanging out with me that day.

"Oh, you guys think there's something funny goin' on here?" Dad snapped, after abruptly stopping his count.

Dean, who wasn't about to "smack the bear on the nose," wisely assumed a little more subdued demeanor, by quickly replying, "No sir...nothing funny at all!"

On the other hand, Mack, being two years older and not as easily "cowed," answered rather boisterously, "I ain't laughin' 'cause I think it's funny. I'm laughin' 'cause it looks like fun!"

Needless to say, that turned out to be the wrong answer!

"Well, then...in that case, both of you feel free to jump right in here and join the "party!" It'd sure be impolite of us to be havin' all this "fun," and leave you guys out!" Dad replied sarcastically and, at the same time, hilariously.

I just glanced down at the ground and quietly chuckled, as I could just see Dean rolling his eyes and shaking his head at his older brother's remark. Because, unlike his more athletic sibling, Dean abhorred anything that would make him have to run, jump or sweat. In fact, my cousin was, and still is, the most energy efficient human I've ever known. And no...that's not a polite way of inferring that he was lazy, because Dean became very skilled and productive as an adult.

But regardless, the two boys formed a line behind me, while Dad instructed them to watch closely what I was doing and try to follow along. He then resumed his cadence…but, this time, at a much faster pace. After about ten minutes into the jumping jacks, the sound of the breathing behind me began getting louder and louder. Unfortunately for them, they weren't given any time to catch that breath, when Dad immediately ordered us to the ground, and to begin performing push-ups. Then, as soon as they were completed, we were ordered to our feet and to start running in place.

I knew what was coming next, and although I was totally exhausted, a little smile began forming of my face. When Dad suddenly shouted, "Down!" I hit the ground flat on my stomach, followed by the sound of two loud "thuds" coming from behind me. This signaled the beginning of the dreaded "grass drills" that Dad had recently begun closing my exercise session with. And, as was standard order of procedure with this routine, the "Down!" was quickly followed by an "Up!" while the "trainee" continued running in place. After only a few rounds into the exercise, the loud "thuds" behind me were soon replaced by the sound of footsteps…fast ones…that rapidly became fainter and fainter.

Still lying on my stomach, I began laughing so hard that I was unable to get to my feet when Dad, once again, shouted, "Up!" But I didn't have to, because I soon heard him laughing, also… followed by, "Go on back inside. We're done!"

Oftentimes, when Dad would be giving me an unusually hard time, Joan would come out and start doing the exercises with me, and that would sort of calm him down a little. And on more than one occasion, I would hear Mom yell out the window for him to,

"Stop being so hard on the boy!" But mostly, I was left to my own resources, which was simply trying to block the pain and fatigue from my mind...and just survive one more day!

It was also during this time that I got to go on my first rabbit hunt. Dad had given me a toy shotgun for my sixth birthday, the first day of November, and I was just itching to try it out. It came complete with stoppers attached to short, thin chains that shot from the barrels when the triggers were pulled, creating a "popping" sound. By that time, I had grown bored with the imaginary game animals I had been "shooting," so you can imagine how excited I was when Dad asked me if I would like to go with him and his brother, Pat, on the first hunt of the season.

Back then, rabbit and upland bird seasons began on Thanksgiving Day. Mom was already busy preparing a big holiday meal, so they planned on just hunting behind our house, instead of driving way out into the country, as was usually the custom. And before you ask, yes, you could go farther back into the country than where we lived...but you'd better pack a lunch!

As the three of us began making our way down to the old grownover fields and thickets below our property, with the pack of beagles running eagerly in front, I was so excited my hands were trembling. And I almost peed in my pants when Dad suddenly yelled out, "There he goes!" after a rabbit bounded out from underneath a brush pile he'd jumped up and down on.

When he began calling the dogs to put them on the trail, Uncle Pat told me to come with him. He knew the rabbit would be running in large circles, so he was going to find a good location to wait for its return. That turned out to be an old tractor road, which ran between an overgrown pasture and a thick stand of small field pines.

With the baying of the dogs growing louder and louder, I raised my gun to my shoulder when I saw Uncle Pat do the same with his. My heart was beating so loud I could hear it when the rabbit suddenly sprang from the pasture and into the little road. Stopping just long enough to figure out which direction to take, it finally saw my uncle and me and wisely began running in the opposite direction. However, the bunny had only made a couple long strides, when Uncle Pat and I, simultaneously, pulled our triggers.

With a loud roar, lead and smoke blasted from the barrel of Uncle Pat's gun, completely drowning out the little "pop" from mine. Still yet, the stoppers headed straight for their target, and the rabbit turned several flips in the air before coming to rest in the middle of the road. That's right, I gave him both barrels. With the corks swinging to and fro from the end of my gun, I just stood there for several seconds, stunned at what I had witnessed. Then I began quickly running for the downed rabbit, all the while shouting, "I got him! I got him!"

I had just held the rabbit up for Uncle Pat to see when the beagles suddenly emerged from the pasture and knocked me to the ground. As they began sniffing excitedly at their quarry, my uncle quickly pulled it from my hand and led the aroused pack away. After getting back on my feet, I heard Uncle Pat laughing and began wondering what he thought was so funny.

"And just what makes you think it was you that got him?" he asked, finally revealing the reason for his immense amusement.

"Because when I shot, I saw the feathers fly!" I proudly replied.

All of a sudden, it was my uncle's turn to drop to the ground, then over on his back, as his laughter grew even louder.

When Dad finally came walking up the road, he took one

look at his brother, then turned to me and asked, "What's Pat laughing at?"

Still staring curiously at my uncle, I just slowly shook my head and answered, "I guess he'd never seen a little kid shoot a rabbit before."

With both my uncle and dad now roaring with laughter, I snatched the rabbit from Uncle Pat's hand, shouldered my shotgun, and went running back to the house to show my prize to Mom.

And Dean told me that I would be totally remiss, if I failed to include this little "jewel" in my book…although I probably shouldn't. However, he seemed to think it was particularly funny, so here goes.

Remember that wooden bench I told you about, earlier…the one my father constructed for us kids to sit on at the kitchen table? Great, I thought you would! And I guess he built the bench for no other reason than it would be much easier to do that, than to build three separate chairs…chairs that we kids would soon outgrow. Now do you see where I got my "cleverness" from?

The backless bench was situated along the outer kitchen wall, directly in front of the windows. My mother sat alone at the opposite side of the table, allowing her easier access to the stove, while Dad, of course, sat at the head of the table, to Mom's left. Now, the seating arrangement for us kids is very important here. Joan sat on the end of the bench nearest Dad, with Alvin at the other end. That left me in the middle, and there was very sound reasoning behind this, other than simply the order of our births… well, at least for me, there was.

I'm sure most of you have heard the old joke about how to tell which one is the "cowboy" when three guys are riding together in the front seat of a pickup truck. Of course, the answer is the one seated in the middle, because he doesn't have to drive, and he also doesn't have to get out to close the gate.

Well, I suppose I've always had a little cowboy in me. Besides not having to be disturbed if I were seated at one end, and the one seated in the middle decided to get up from the table, there happened to be another, more important, advantage. You see, between the two windows was a one-foot wide section of wall that made a perfect backrest.

It appears that Joan always envied my more favorable seating position, and was often seen leaning against the window directly behind her…much to Dad's displeasure. And he was always warning her that she was going to fall through it one day. Of course, Joan being Joan, always gave him the standard response, "No I'm not! Do you think I'm stupid?" And as we all know, one should never tempt Fate!

It just so happened that Dean was spending some time with my family, as his mother was in the hospital having a baby that had to be delivered through Cesarean section. This meant his stay with us turned out to be longer than anticipated. So he was seated at the foot of the table one morning at breakfast, in a big chair that Dad had brought up from the basement. And Dean, being the little fellow he was, looked plum comical sitting in it. But that's not what made the story I'm telling so funny…although it certainly helped!

For some reason that I don't recall now, my sister had to get up from the table for a few minutes. And while she was gone, it seems it became a little too warm in the house for Dad, with it being early summer and my mom had had a hot fire burning in our kitchen stove. So naturally, he got up and opened both windows.

Now what could possibly go wrong with this scenario?

Well, when Joan finally returned, the first thing she did was pick up her glass of milk and lean back against the window. Needless to say, we all know that window was no longer down, so my sister kept going backward until her back met the screen. Unfortunately, the screen was in pretty bad shape, and immediately we heard a sharp, ripping sound. Now with Alvin and me having our backs toward the point of interest, Dean suddenly had the best seat in the house! And here's how he described what happened next:

He said Joan did a complete flip in the air, hit the ground running, and was back in the house before Mom could get to the back door! And knowing how lithe and athletic my sister was back then, I have no doubts that what he recounted was completely accurate.

But even with milk covering her face and running down her blouse, Joan remained her unflappable self. After calmly retaking her seat, she just looked around at all of us howling with laughter, then indignantly asked, "What's so darn funny?"

And to this day, my sister still maintains that Dad opened that window, *hoping* she'd fall through it, thinking it might teach her a lesson. And I suppose that was definitely a possibility...maybe a lesson like, in this particular instance, "Pride goeth before a fall." I know, that was way too easy. But, anyway, we all know my dad would *never* do anything like that.

And how could I forget that morning, the following winter, when dear old Santa gave me my most favorite Christmas present ever! I was awakened deep in the night by the sound of the front door opening and closing, and peeked underneath the door, only to notice that the living room light was on. Even though it had taken me forever to fall asleep, knowing what was awaiting us kids when morning came, I was now wide awake.

Hearing the muffled knocking and banging taking place, then a "shhhh…be quiet!" coming from my mother, made me want to climb out of bed and run right in there.

But Mom had told me, while tucking us in that night, not to get up until she and Dad came to get us. So I just lay back down and listened attentively.

I realized our fireplace had been covered over and a wood-burning stove placed in front of it, so Mom or Dad had to have let Santa in through the front door. But I still couldn't understand why she would be acting so "bossy" toward him. After all, if he was as fat as some of the pictures I'd seen of him, he couldn't help but make a little racket…especially, if he was carrying that big bag I always saw him with! Nevertheless, I just lay patiently in bed until I finally heard the door open and Mom yell out, "Are you guys awake yet?"

My mother barely got out of the doorway in time to avoid getting "plowed under," as I barreled my way through it, with Alvin right on my heels! However, after entering the living room, I couldn't help but feel a little disappointment when I noticed Joan already kneeling at the bottom of the tree, opening her present. Then, I suddenly had to rub my eyes in disbelief when I saw what was on the other side of that tree. For there, appearing almost magical in the dim Christmas lights, were two of the most beautiful bicycles I had ever seen!

One of them was painted red, and was a little larger than the other, orange one…so I ran straight for the red bike! But when I grabbed hold of it, and began pushing it from beneath the tree, I noticed something odd hanging from the handle bars. Bound together and then tied to the bike with string…I'm sure as a reminder of what a "bad boy" I had been that year…were several hickory switches!

"How could he?" I thought to myself. "How could Santa do this to me…especially, after all I've been through?" I then looked up at Mom, and when I saw that she was smiling and nodding toward my father, my disdain quickly "zeroed" in on him.

"It figures," I thought to myself. "He couldn't even allow me one happy day out of the whole dang year!"

However, this incident did present me with a very valuable life lesson. And that was, no matter how beautiful and desirable something appears to be when it enters your life, look it over very carefully to make sure there's no strings attached. Uh, well…not that I've ever learned that lesson.

But anyway, that's how it was with the mysterious, little puppy. Before that Christmas Day of 1955, he had entered and departed my life three times. And on each occasion, I ignored the obvious "strings" that were attached to him, simply because I didn't want to see them. The little pup filled my heart with an unimaginable joy, at a time when I needed it most. So, to me, that was all that mattered. But because of circumstances beyond my control, he was taken from me each time, leaving my emotions in a state of total devastation.

For several months, I kept a constant vigil, waiting for Shep's return. But as more and more days passed, without any sign of him, I began to slowly lose hope that I would ever see him again. On more than one occasion, I wanted to just say, "To heck with it!" and march straight to the Haskins house to check on him. But I realized this would only cause me, and him, even more heartbreak when I had to leave there without him. So I just accepted the way things were and tried to "trudge" along without him, the best I could.

Then, on a beautiful spring morning, I think some time around mid-April, I was sitting in the front porch swing, pondering these very things and recalling how horrible my life had become. When, all of a sudden, my "pity party" was suddenly brought to a dramatic close. For out of the corner of my eye, a flash of sable and white caught my attention, and when I turned my head to determine what it was, I couldn't believe what I was seeing. There, running across our front yard and toward me, at a full gallop, came a beautiful adult collie!

"Could that be Shep?" I thought, jumping out of the swing and running down the steps. Then, when the dog bounded into my arms, knocking me to the ground, and began licking my face, I knew it had to be! That adorable little puppy, who was only twelve weeks old when I last saw him, was now a six month-old adult…and the most splendid creature I had ever seen! As soon as I was able to get back on my feet, I went running into the house, screaming, "Mama, Mama, Shep's come home!"

However, Mom, who was standing at the kitchen sink washing our breakfast dishes, didn't appear to share the same joy and excitement that I was exhibiting. Instead, she just shook her head as her normal pleasant expression suddenly turned into one of consternation and worry.

Wiping her hands on her apron, she grabbed me by the shoulders and softly admonished, "Hush! You're going to wake up your dad!"

"He already has!" we suddenly heard coming from the back bedroom. And when I heard the door open, I prudently decided that my time might be better served outside of the house.

Making a hasty retreat back through the front door, I rejoined Shep on the porch, who was anxiously prancing back and forth, awaiting my return. I knelt down and threw my arms around his neck, but when I did, I again noticed something peculiar on his neck. Just behind his ears were two raw, bloody swaths where there should have been hair.

"Well, it looks like they had him tied again," Dad commented, after walking out the door and squatting down next to me.

As he gently rubbed his thumb across one of the wounds, he further surmised, "I guess ol' Charley put him on a chain this time, so the dog couldn't chew it in two. But, instead, he's pulled and pulled until he finally got his head through the collar."

Almost moved to tears by Dad's description of what Shep had been suffering through over the past months, I pleaded, "Can we do something for him? I know that's got to hurt!"

"Yeah, I have a little something that should fix him right up," he replied. "Bring him 'round to the back yard."

Following my father's instructions, I was waiting with Shep at the rear steps when he walked out the back door carrying a blue bottle. I immediately recognized it as his much "renowned" *Blue Star Ointment,* widely celebrated among the more astute "dog men" of the day, for curing any type of cut, scrape or sore occurring to their hounds. It seems I remember him telling me once, that you could even drink it for snake bite. He said that it wouldn't do a damn bit of good for the bite, but if you drank enough of the stuff, it'd sure make you forget about the pain!

As Dad was massaging the elixir into Shep's festering sores, I was almost afraid to ask him what was on my mind…worried about the answer I might get. Finally summoning enough courage, I blurted out, "Daddy, don't you think I ought to be able to keep him this time?" He's just gonna keep trying to get loose if they take him back. And I just couldn't stand to think about this happening to him again!"

Then, with my anger finally getting the better of me, I wiped the tears from my eyes and emphatically stated, "Damn it, he's been through enough!"

Dad just looked at me for several seconds…I'm sure, because he'd never heard me cuss before…then said, "And I guess you have, too. No, they're not gittin' the dog back!"

My anger was still "boiling" over, a couple weeks later, when Shep and I were rolling around together in the front yard. All of a sudden, he stopped playing, turned to face the road and began emitting a low growl. When I stood to see what had caught his attention, I heard those familiar voices echoing down the road. My first impulse was to run with him to the back yard. Then I remembered what Dad had said, so I just stood my ground.

I'm sure we made a strange sight when the two girls finally got close enough to our yard to see us. They immediately stopped talking and began slowing their pace. Then Betty looked at Mule and giggled, when she saw me standing there with both fists balled up, and Shep right next to me, growling.

"Daddy said you can keep that dog!" Betty suddenly yelled out. Then the sisters resumed their original pace and chattering.

Stunned, I just stood there looking at them…but I did relax my fists. That was the last thing I expected to hear, so I didn't know how to react. Finally, I gave them a meek, "Thanks," but they were almost all the way to Johnsie and Ozelle's house, by then.

That night, as I lay in my bed, with Shep lying on his mat outside my window, I began my nightly prayers.

"Thank you God for my family. Thank you God for allowing me to come home from that awful hospital. Thank you God for helping me make it through my exercises, and for any good they may be doing me. Thank you God for finding a way for Shep and me to stay together."

Then, pausing for a moment, I took a deep breath and whispered with even more sincerity, "And thank God, I didn't have to slug it out with Mule!"

No Ordinary Dog

With Shep now being a full-time member of the Crawley household, it wasn't long until the others in my family finally realized what I knew all along; there was something very special about that dog! They got the first indication of this after one of our evening meals.

Mom always threw our table scraps and leftovers into an old metal bucket, which Dad kept in a narrow, screened-in foyer that served as our back porch. Every evening, usually right after supper, he would add enough dry dog feed to fill the bucket, then head to the dog lot to give his seven or eight beagles their daily meal. On the way there, he would stop at a six-foot square concrete well cover and place a large scoop of it into an old metal plate, which served as Shep's food dish.

This daily routine had only been taking place for about a week, when Dad walked out the backdoor with his feed bucket one evening to a big surprise. Shep was standing at the bottom of the steps, holding the plate between his teeth. Apparently, he had heard my father mixing the scraps and feed together, and thought he would help speed up the process.

"Sue, come here and look at this," I heard Dad call out to Mom. Of course, I was right behind her when she walked out the kitchen door.

"My Lord, I had no idea he was that smart!" she exclaimed, as I just stood next to her smiling proudly.

However, I had already witnessed Shep doing things that were even more incredible, so I didn't see what all the fuss was about. A short time later, I did ask Dad how smart he thought my dog was, since he pretty much knew more about them than anyone around.

After scratching his head and thinking about it for several seconds, he finally replied, "Ah, he's purty smart, I reckon...but not nearly as smart as a couple of the beagles I have."

However, it wasn't but a short while later, when he was forced to re-evaluate his opinion.

He and Mom were sitting in the porch swing one pleasant June evening, just as the sun was beginning to set. We kids were running around in the front yard trying to catch the fireflies, which were just beginning to make their nightly appearance. Shep started out participating in this fun activity with us, but evidently grew bored and decided to go sit on the porch with my parents and just watch.

Eventually, Alvin, who was only four at the time, saw one near the road and went chasing after it. No one noticed this until a car came speeding down the highway. With darkness settling in and the car not running its headlights, it was a catastrophe just waiting to happen.

"Joan, go get Alvin!" Mom screamed, when she finally noticed what was taking place.

Immediately, my sister went running after her little brother but, as it turned out, there was really no need. Before she had taken more than a couple strides, Shep flew right past her and latched on to the back of Alvin's shorts, just as he was about to enter the road. With the car's horn blaring, the dog just stood there holding on until Joan could take him by the hand and lead him back to the house.

Mom, who had only made it about half way across the yard, was holding both hands over her mouth, unable to speak, when Joan handed Alvin over to her.

"I cannot believe what I just saw!" she finally stated, after regaining her composure.

Kneeling down and placing an arm around Shep's neck, I looked over at my father, then back up at Mom, before snidely remarking, "Oh, didn't Dad tell you? He's got a couple beagles that would've done the same thing!"

Saving Alvin that summer evening was just the first of Shep's many heroics that come to mind when I think back on his time with us. However, when it came to me, his protective instincts took on almost epic proportions. The first incident I recall, happened on a hot and sultry July day in 1955. It may seem minor in comparison to some of the other amazing exploits he performed later on, but it was the first time I realized just how much I meant to Shep...and just how much he meant to me.

Dean had come over that day to play with Alvin and me, but after trying our best to ignore the abnormally high temperature and humidity, my cousin came up with a tantalizing remedy to the oppressive heat.

"Hey, why don't we go down to the big creek...the one on the

Tallent property?" he suggested with a big smile lighting up his face.

Although it sounded like a good idea while sitting in the shade of the big willow tree, wiping sweat from our sunburned faces, I wasn't so sure Mom would feel the same. The small stream, located just a couple hundred feet below our property line, was as far as we were allowed to go without permission. However, this much larger one was almost a half mile beyond that. And unlike the smaller stream, where we could only wade around in ankle-deep water, the one Dean had in mind was deep enough to completely immerse our bodies.

"It sounds good, but I don't think Mama will let us go down there," I replied.

"Why would she even have to know?" Dean shot right back.

As I just sat there staring at him, wrestling with the decision I was attempting to make, Dean continued "casting his bait."

"We'll just run down there, jump in, and jump right back out. Your mama won't even know we're gone. And just think about how cold that water is!"

That third "cast" was the last one my cousin needed to make, for me to "swallow his bait hook, line and sinker!" But, of course, Dean could've made a very comfortable living selling tropical vacations to the residents of Tahiti.

"Okay, if you think we can pull it off," I answered, finally acquiescing, though still a bit apprehensive. "Let me run inside first, and see what Mama's doing."

After entering the house through the back door, I noticed Mom standing at the sink, filling her mop bucket with water.

"Do you need something?" she asked when I hesitated for just a moment, before turning back around to leave.

"Uh…well…I just wanted a drink of water," I stammered.

"Can you get one from the outside spigot?" she asked. "I'll be here a while."

"Yeah…okay, I will." I replied, then walked quickly back out the door.

Knowing my mother would be busy mopping the floors for the next hour or so, I gave the all-clear signal while running down the steps. Immediately, the four of us, which included Shep, went scurrying for the woods at the lower end of our property. After crossing the little, meandering branch, we went about a hundred yards farther to a large soybean field. This marked the nearest boundary of the Tallent farm. There, we picked up a little tractor road, which led us to the small creek…and "liquid Heaven!"

After hastily peeling off both our shorts and underwear, so that nothing would be wet when we returned home, we then made a wild, "buck-naked" dash for the cool, refreshing water. And boy, did it feel good…so good, in fact, that we lost all track of time! So much for the "jump right in, and right back out!" sale's pitch Dean had given me!

Finally realizing that our little "excursion" had taken way longer than our original plan, I immediately got out of the water and began putting my shorts back on. Once Dean and Alvin had done the same, we went "hightailing" it back to the house as fast as we could run. But that run came to a dead stop, when we got within sight of the barn and saw Mom standing there…without her "smiley face."

The old adage of "spare the rod and spoil the child" may have become somewhat out of touch in today's politically correct society, but back then, especially in my household, it was very much adhered to. So Alvin and I, very reluctantly, began a slow "death march" to our mother who stood directly in our path with a scowl on her face and Dad's belt in her hand.

I just shook my head in disgust when Dean gave me and my brother a quick, "See you guys," then made a large half circle around Mom.

Although I didn't reply to him out loud, I was wishing he could've heard the, "Sure thing…and thanks a lot, A-hole!" that was running through my head.

Mama walked right past me and went straight for Alvin. He had already begun to cry, so three or four firm lashes across his bare legs was all it took to send him running to the house, wailing in pain.

Now, it was just Mom and me! And knowing that she thought I had been the instigator of this little caper, I also knew I wasn't about to get off nearly as easily as my younger brother.

"I know this was all your idea…and I knew you were up to something when you came in the house for water, instead of getting it outside like you normally would," she began lecturing me. "Do you know how long I've been walking around in those woods, calling for you kids?"

I knew that, "Could I have 20,000 guesses?" wouldn't be a well-advised and judicious response to Mom's rhetorical question…but knowing what was coming next, I must admit, I certainly did consider it!

So, with nothing to say that would appreciably sway Mom's judgement…or alter, in any meaningful way, my punishment…I just silently shook my head and braced myself for the inevitable.

Still steaming with anger, my mother grabbed me by the arm, then raised the belt. But before it came crashing down against my legs, I heard a loud bark…then nothing!

After slowly opening my eyes, I couldn't believe what I was seeing! Shep was standing defiantly between my mother and me, growling ferociously...with the belt clinched firmly between his teeth.

Becoming even more enraged, Mama jerked the belt from his mouth, then yelled at him to stand down. Never one to disobey a command, Shep obediently, but slowly, backed away. However, he kept staring intensely at her.

Once again, Mom grabbed my arm and started to swing the belt, and once again, Shep leaped for it and jerked it from her grasp! This time, after taking it back, Mom directed her blow at Shep, striking him hard across his face.

"Mama, don't!" I screamed, dropping to my knees and throwing my arms around the loyal dog's neck.

Then, after getting back on my feet, I yelled at her, "Don't hit my dog! You can hit me all you want...but don't ever hit my dog again!"

With tears now streaming down my face, I walked over to the barn and opened the door. Then, turning to Mom, I said, "Whip me in here...away from Shep."

After she came inside and shut the door, I turned my back to her, then braced myself for the stinging blows I knew would follow. But they never came! Instead, I heard the door swing back open. Turning around to see what was taking place, I was shocked to see my mother walking back outside.

"That damn dog!" was all I heard her say, as she began making her way back to the house.

It wasn't just Mom who experienced Shep's profound loyalty when it came to protecting me. Only a couple weeks later, it was my father's turn to witness, first hand, just what extremes Shep would go to when he thought my safety was threatened.

Joan and I had spent the better part of a day erecting a tent from two old, threadbare bed sheets Mom had given us. Proud of our achievement, we asked if it would be okay for the two of us… and Alvin, if he wanted…to camp out in the back yard that night, so we could really put it to use.

"Oh, I don't think there'd be a problem with that," she responded. "But you'll have to wait until your dad gets up this evening, and check with him, too."

As usual, our father was in a pretty cranky mood after walking out of his bedroom, so that was something neither of us looked forward to. All during supper, my sister and I kept punching each other in the ribs, trying to goad the other into popping the question. However, it was Mom, after recognizing what was going on, who finally broke the stalemate.

"Long, the kids want to spend the night in their tent, in the back yard," she spoke up.

"What damn tent?" he grumpily inquired.

"They made one out of a couple old bed sheets I threw away," Mom informed him.

Joan and I held our breaths as Dad just glanced over at us, pensively shaking his head. I should probably mention that this was taking place on a Friday evening, which meant he didn't have to go in to work that night. So we were hoping that would factor, favorably, in his decision. Still yet, we were both floored when he finally gave us his answer.

"Why not? Let 'em get a little taste of what I went through in North Africa…minus the damn flies!" he growled.

Flies or no flies, we were overjoyed with what we'd just heard, and began running excitedly for the back door, even though neither of us knew where the heck North Africa was!

With help from Mom, Joan and I spent the remainder of the evening getting the makeshift tent ready for a sleepover. Our mother placed a couple old quilts, along with our pillows, on the ground for padding. Then, she spread a blanket over them for us to climb under when it became considerably cooler toward the morning.

Around nine-thirty, Joan and I were finally settled in for the night, along with Alvin and Shep. Mama climbed inside one final time to make sure we were comfortably tucked in, and to give us a flashlight. After a goodnight kiss for each of us kids, and a pat on the head for Shep, she closed the front opening with several clothespins, then started back to the house. We then heard the back door open, just as she was about to climb the steps, and Dad's voice.

"Where's the dog?" he asked her.

After a brief hesitation, Mom reluctantly answered, "He's in the tent."

"Good god almighty!" Dad fumed, as he started down the steps.

After hastily undoing the tent opening, he railed, "Get that dog out of there! You'll have fleas and ticks all over your beddin'!"

Once Shep was brusquely escorted from the tent, I just scratched my head and thought, "Geesh, they must not have had any of those things in North Africa!"

As we lay there listening, somewhat nervously, to the many strange night sounds around us, Joan suggested that we tell ghost stories to pass the time until we fell asleep. This had always been a popular activity in our house…well, until we finally acquired a television set, several months earlier. Although the old "hand-me-down" tales, verbalized to us by Mom and Dad, had become all too familiar by now, they still aroused plenty of fear… especially, when told in the unfamiliar setting we were now in. Enough so, that Alvin bolted from the tent and made a mad dash to the house, just a few minutes in to them.

As he began screaming and banging on the backdoor, Joan and I just laughed…that is, until Dad opened it and yelled, "What the hell's goin' on out there?"

Then, when he started down the steps, we quickly ducked under the blanket.

"I guess you smart alecks think it's real funny scarin' your little brother like that?" he quipped.

"We were just telling ghost stories. We weren't trying to scare him," Joan replied.

"Oh, so you two like ghost stories, huh?" Dad mused with a mischievous little laugh, as he knelt to reclose the tent opening.

Before starting back to the house, he looked down at Shep, who was now lying at the front of the tent, and asked, "Why did you bring his mat around here?"

I poked my head out a small opening to see what my father was talking about, and to my surprise, discovered that Shep was lying on the sleeping mat that we kept on the front porch for him.

"I didn't bring it around here!" I finally stated.

"Well, it didn't git here by itself!" he countered.

Joan then settled the matter by explaining, "Oh yeah! Don't you remember hearing him dragging something right before we started telling the ghost stories? That must've been what it was!"

Dad just stared down at Shep for several seconds, shaking his head…I'm sure, in amazement at the dog's cleverness…then, headed back to the house.

After everything had calmed back down, Joan and I soon fell fast asleep…but, unfortunately, it didn't last long. Suddenly, we were awakened by a low growl coming from Shep. Joan immediately reached for the flashlight and flipped it on. As we strained our ears to try to determine what had caught his attention, we suddenly heard a low moaning sound coming from the far corner of the house. In a flash, my sister and I, again, ducked under the blanket. Just a second or two later, Shep let loose a loud, threatening bark, then went charging toward the strange sound.

Frozen rigid in fear, Joan and I were unable to move. But when a horrific fight began taking place, with fierce snarls and growls intermingled with shouts of profanity, I could no longer remain where I was and do nothing. Fearing for Shep's safety, I grabbed the flashlight from my sister, bolted from the tent and went running toward the vicious melee.

However, I was once again paralyzed with fear when I shined the flashlight on the frightening disturbance and finally saw what was taking place. Just a few yards away, perched atop the shoulders of what appeared to be some type of headless apparition, was Shep! And even more surreal, he was biting ferociously at the opening where a head should've been!

Fortunately, just as I was about to pass out from fear, I heard Dad's voice coming from inside the strange creature, yelling, "Get this damn dog off of me!"

I immediately called for Shep, who begrudgingly jumped down and came back to the tent. He then took up a defensive position in front of me, still growling at his unknown adversary. Then, in an abrupt change of emotion, I almost fell to my knees laughing when Dad began unbuttoning his old army pea coat. It had a really wide collar, which he had closed around his head…

thusly, creating the "decapitated monster" that had scared the "holy bejesus" out of Joan and me.

"Git all of that bedding, along with your sorry butts, back inside the house!" he indignantly demanded, after removing the overcoat and starting up the steps.

Mom, who had witnessed the entire event unfold…but as an innocent bystander, of course…came out the door just as Dad was going in. She tried hard to suppress her laughter as she passed by him but, nonetheless, began laughing uproariously after he'd gone inside. And it continued the whole time she was helping Joan and me gather up our bedroll. In fact, I could still hear her snickering, from time to time, long after we were tucked in our beds.

Old Bess

As you can probably imagine, with occurrences like the ones I just described taking place on a regular basis, we very quickly realized Shep wasn't your typical, run-of-the-mill "pot-licker." And not too long afterward, an even more incredible incident took place that caused many of our neighbors to realize this, as well. But before I get too far ahead of myself, let me return one final time to the period immediately after the Haskins had relinquished possession of that blessed and divine dog to me.

I'm sure you've noticed by now that not long after my bout with polio, I was physically strong enough to keep up with my peers in the running and playing department. This was due mostly to Dad's strict and strenuous exercise regimen. However, I don't think it would have been nearly as successful without the contributions Shep had made to my mental and emotional health.

You see, before he was around full time, I was simply "treading water," as far as achieving any goals set forth in my daily workout regimen. And no matter how much my father berated and chastised me, I stubbornly refused to put any more effort into them than was absolutely necessary, in order to keep him placated. Because, at that juncture in my life, the future appeared so bleak and hopeless that I considered it futile and foolish to make it any more difficult than it already was.

What I, or no one, knew at the time, was that I had developed full-blown clinical depression from my time at the hospital, separated from my parents, home and loved ones...especially, at such a young age. We saw it with children who were recently removed from the custody of their parents and loved ones at the Mexican border, even though many child psychologists were warning federal agents and government officials about the tremendous harm and lasting effects they were subjecting these children to. And many of them were much older than I was, at the time of my separation. If I appear to be making a political statement here, I'm not. I'm just stating facts!

But when Shep came along, he quickly began turning my gloom into happiness, while replacing much of my despair with hope…not to mention, a newly acquired sense of belonging and self-worth. After all, if something as pure and simple as a dog could love me that much, then surely, there must be enough inherent value within me to make my life worth living.

Yeah, I know. This book is starting to get a little sappy again. So, with that being said, it might be a good time to turn off the "violin music" for a while, and start telling you guys about that other incredible thing Shep did.

But before I do, I'd like to reiterate, one final time, my state of mind at the time of this latest incident. Although I still had to deal with all of the same obstacles and hurdles I'd been presented with, I wasn't worrying about them nearly as much as before.

Shep's presence had built a wall, so to speak, between me and my worries, allowing my confidence and optimism to now become stronger than my fears and doubts.

So, I guess you could say that I had begun putting all of my many travails into a more proper perspective. Not the least of which, was the sound of Dad's car turning in to our driveway on week-day mornings, announcing the painful ordeal that would soon follow. I now realized the more effort and enthusiasm I put into my exercises, the quicker they'd be over. And the sooner they were over, the more time I had to spend with Shep. Heck, I now found myself doing extra rounds of them after my dad had turned in for the day. That's right, on my own, and without any arm-twisting and coercion from the "Sergeant Carter" wannabe! Oh, come on! I know y'all watched Gomer Pile, U.S.M.C.!

Anyway, that's what I was doing on that spring day in 1957. We were out of school for Easter break, so I was in the backyard doing some chin-ups on the bar Dad had put in the willow tree. I was also keeping a close eye on Old Bess. You remember her…the dairy cow with an attitude? She had just delivered her first calf a couple days earlier, and it was the cutest thing I'd ever seen. The problem was…I always had this really strong weakness for "cute!"

Dad had told us kids, just the day before, not to go inside the pasture. He said if we thought Bess was mean before, she'd be twice as ornery now. I have no idea why, but although he was addressing all three of us at the time, he kept looking straight at me.

After dropping from the chin-up bar, I walked over to the fence and gazed out across the pasture at the newly-born calf. I'd never seen one up close before, and wondered what it would feel like to pet the little fellow. He was just lying on the ground taking a nap, while his mother continued to graze farther and farther away from him.

About this time, Mom came out the back door carrying a basket of dirty laundry. As she headed for the old wringer washing machine in the basement, a thought suddenly popped into my head. There were no windows down there…and with Dad in bed, fast asleep…no one would know if I went inside the pasture to pet that little guy.

When Mom opened the basement door, Shep, who had been lying beneath the tree, got up and followed her inside. It was a pretty warm day, and he liked laying down there on the cool floor. Suddenly finding myself alone, I turned my attention back to the calf. In doing so, I noticed that Bess was now about fifty yards from her baby, almost all the way to the other side of the pasture. If I were going to do this, now would be my best opportunity.

I don't mean to keep you in suspense, but before I delve any further into this story, I should probably fill you in on a little more of Old Bess's history.

Dad had purchased the cow, the previous fall, from a friend of his since childhood, named John Doe. Of course, that wasn't his real name, but I'll explain the reasoning behind that after just a few more paragraphs.

I'm having difficulty remembering if my father actually paid Mr. Doe for her, or if the man simply gave the cow to him. Anyway, if money was exchanged, it wasn't very much…and you're probably beginning to understand why!

The Doe's resided about five miles from where we lived, and just a "skip and a hop" from where my dad grew up. I recall our family often visiting them on Sunday afternoons, although I never really liked going there, and would rather have milked a female mountain lion than to do it. Although Mr. and Mrs. Doe were very nice people from what I remember, they had two kids, a son and a daughter, who were straight out of the Sunday morning funny pages...especially, the pudgy, rat-faced boy! And to make matters worse, neither he nor his older sister cared anything at all for my siblings and me. So they seemed to revel in teasing and playing mean tricks on us, at every opportunity. And the rest of the time, they settled for just being unsociable, miscreant cretins.

I know you readers are probably thinking, what does this have to do with the "price of beans," or Old Bess, for that matter? Well, actually..............nothing, darn it! But I finally have the opportunity to skewer that pair of arrogant, snotty-nosed, pompous bozos in a book...and I'm damned well going to!

Well, I guess there's no need for me to give you any further explanation as to why I got into such a "rhubarb" with my publisher over this little matter of journalistic freedom, and was reluctantly forced to use a fake name!

Anyhoo...Mr. Doe (sigh) delivered Bess, as my father would later name her, to our house in the bed of his old farm truck. After getting her out, Dad attached a chain to her neck and led her down to a grass-covered field below the house. There, he secured her to a metal stake driven into the ground, so that she would be able to graze. However, he had to relocate her several times a day, after she had grazed out the perimeter around her chain stake.

Bess also had to be led to the little branch below our property, twice a day, to drink. I still remember the first time Dad tried this. Evidently, the old girl wasn't in the mood to be led around on the end of a chain. So when my father began jerking on her, she went charging straight at him with lowered horns. Remember that "beaning" I mentioned earlier? That's when it happened!

The second Dad saw her coming at him, he picked up a two-by-four, conveniently lying on a tarp-covered stack of hay, and proceeded to slap her flat across the forehead with it. Stunned, the cow immediately came to a stop and began wobbling from side to side, as if she were about to tumble over. When I began laughing at her, she cut a mean glare in my direction, then resumed calmly chewing her cud, as if nothing had happened. I have no idea what Bess was thinking during those ten or fifteen seconds…but whatever it was, she never forgot it!

As you've probably already guessed by now, it was pretty challenging, to put it mildly, taking care of Bess without a fenced in pasture and running water, or even a barn to shelter her in. And I'm sure you're also wondering what would possess a person to obtain a cow without any of these amenities, in the first place! Well, maybe I need to tell you a little more about Dad's history, also.

My father hailed from a very self-reliant family that included his parents and seven siblings, whose chief means of feeding themselves consisted almost entirely of subsistence farming. Now, in case any of you young "whippersnappers" need to look that term up on your smart phones, go ahead. See, it was a pretty harsh way to have to live, wasn't it?

Just about all of their furniture was either handmade or hand-me-downs, and a lot of their everyday clothing was hand sewn from whatever fabric they could come by, which usually turned out to be ornately dyed flour sacks. Heck, even what little spending money they generated came mainly from harvesting some of the trees on their property, then transporting them about ten miles, by mule and wagon, to a pulpwood processing yard near Marion. I suppose you could say they lived their lives very much like those Amish families you see on television, but without as many constraints and limitations due to their religious beliefs.

I guess what it all boiled down to is this; my father's old man wasn't the kind of person to go running to a store to pay hard-earned money for something they were perfectly capable of producing themselves. So with my dad being the "chip off the old block" that he was, he certainly wasn't about to pass up an opportunity to own a dairy cow that would provide his family with free milk and butter...pasture or no pasture!

And neither was Dad one to sit idly by, twiddling his thumbs, after finally obtaining that cow. With winter fast approaching, he immediately went to work building a barn for Bess, as well as a dry place to store her hay. Oak trees were cut from the woods just below the future barn site, and positioned atop large stones to serve as the foundation. Mom's brother, Calvin, who was Mack and Dean's father, volunteered his services in aiding Dad with this daunting project.

Once the twenty by fifty foot foundation was in place, my father flattened the top surface with a double-bitted axe, so that eight foot oak uprights could be mounted to it. Then, an oak log top plate was mounted to the upper end of those. He then purchased unfinished oak boards to sheath the outside of the frame.

To complete the barn, he added a hay loft to the front half of the structure and a small stable to the other end. The stable had a three by three foot opening between it and the barn in order to access a hay manger. When the rafters were put in place and covered over by galvanized tin sheets, a beautiful, new barn stood proudly below our house. Well, the ramshackle pile of rough-hewn logs and boards sure looked beautiful to me, and I'm sure they did to Dad, also!

However, that turned out to be the easiest part of turning our little "Dogpatch" homestead into a poor man's dairy farm. Bess would also require a pasture. So Dad went to work, once again, clearing a large section of land for that purpose. But he had to do it without the use of bulldozers, power saws, or any type of mechanized equipment. Nevertheless, this enormous task was somehow accomplished, and all that remained was surrounding the newly cleared pasture with a barbed wire fence, and that's where I entered the picture.

After marking spots on the ground for post holes, most of the digging was left to me. While I struggled with this task, Dad carried over the locust fence posts and laid them out in a line, with one near each hole I was digging. Once the eighteen inch-deep holes were dug, the posts were then set in place and the recently extracted dirt filled back in around them. I then finished the job by tamping in the unpacked soil around the now upright posts with a heavy steel bar. Just guessing, there were probably more than two hundred fence posts that had to be put up, so I'm sure you can imagine what a tired little boy I was at the end of those long days!

But that was only half of the job in erecting a serviceable fence. Once the posts were up, the barbed wire had to be strung. This was accomplished by Dad and me rolling the heavy coils of wire around the perimeter, using a six foot-long pine pole as an axle. Once the wire was laid out, it had to be stretched tight, one post at a time, using only a crow bar for leverage, then nailed in place using inch and a quarter fence staples. And god forbid I allowed the crowbar to slip out of place while my father was pounding the staples into the shaky posts, because I'd get a "cussing" every time! And also keep in mind, all of this had to be done five separate times!

Words can't express how relieved I was after finally concluding three months of the hardest work I've ever done in my life… and how happy Old Bess must have felt to finally be taken off her chain and set free in her new home. Now, in all honesty, I'm not sure if cows even feel happiness, but she certainly felt something, because Bess immediately went about defending her new domain against all intruders, like a wolverine would defend a rotting moose carcass. Well, except for Dad, whom she just barely tolerated.

Nevertheless, this was just a little inconvenience we accepted as a necessary trade-off for Old Bess supplying us with all the milk and butter we could use. In fact, our refrigerator was soon filled to capacity with the commodities. But that allowed Mom to begin selling the surplus, along with eggs, to the neighbors at prices considerably lower than those in the area grocery stores.

However, there happened to be one family living near us who my mother refused to sell her dairy products to. This was the Mann family, who rented an old house just a little more than a stone's throw from ours. Remember when I was categorizing my family's economic status, by saying we were poor, but not "all the way to the bottom" poor? Well, this is the family I used to define the bottom.

The unpainted and deteriorating two-story farmhouse, which provided a home for the two adults and ten children, was within sight of ours, and I went there often to play with the younger boys; Paul, Fred, Collen and Carl. Mr. Mann, the patriarch, was in his late forties or early fifties, but appeared much older. This was due mostly to the frailty of the small-statured man, as well as his stooped-at-the-shoulders posture.

I remember Dad telling me once, that if I didn't start working harder at my exercises, I would someday look just like him. But unlike me, I'm sure the primary reasons for Mr. Mann's less than stellar physical appearance, was his poor diet, coupled with the stress of providing for ten children, while working in a furniture factory, with a bad back, for "starvation" wages. Let's see…did I miss anything? No, I think that about covered it.

However, Mrs. Mann, by way of comparison, had it much harder, if that's even possible! The saintly lady cared for her children with a degree of love and devotion that would've made the Pope smile…and under conditions so impoverished and destitute that it would've made Mother Teresa weep.

I remember being over there on one occasion while the lady was doing the family's laundry. It was a very hot day and she had a fire burning underneath a cast iron kettle, sitting atop three large rocks. I just watched in disbelief as she laboriously drew water from an old well to fill the large pot, then placed the family's few clothes inside it as the water came to a boil.

Even more pitiful, the poor woman was forced to sit in a rickety straight chair, right up against the flames, while tediously scrubbing each individual garment on a washboard so archaic and primitive that it made my mother's old, outdated Sears wringer washing machine look like space-age technology. All the while, the sweet and dedicated lady intermittingly wiped torrents of sweat from her weathered brow onto a tattered, work-stained apron, while singing the words to a Christian hymn. All I can further add…as I wipe these tears from my eyes…is, "May God bless that grand and noble woman. I know her reward was great!"

Later that same evening, Mrs. Mann invited me to stay for supper. Not wanting to appear rude, I graciously accepted.

However, I quickly regretted my decision when I saw what was being served…but only out of guilt that I was depriving them of food they badly needed. Almost in tears, I had to force myself to eat the meager strip of fried fatback pork, served with a small piece of cornbread and washed down with a glass of water. For dessert, they all got a tablespoon of molasses…which I respectfully declined.

Up until then, I thought the reason the younger children had protruding stomachs, was because they were well fed. But I later realized it was the result of malnutrition. Even some of the older ones had boils and sores on their bodies, which never seemed to heal because of their severely weakened immune systems. However, all of that was only superficial and confined to their physical bodies. On the inside, all of those kids possessed the souls of angels…qualities that none of my other friends could come close to matching, and certainly not me!

When I returned home that evening, I was in a pretty sad state of mind…to put it mildly. So I sat down on the front steps for a while, to kind of get my emotions back in check before going inside. But I could never keep anything from Mom, so she soon noticed me sitting there with my face pressed, dejectedly, against Shep's shoulder.

"Is something wrong?" she asked, after stepping out the front door and sitting down next to me.

"Oh no…nothing," I half-heartedly replied, then began stroking the back of my dog's head.

"Are you sure you didn't get in a fight with one of the Mann boys?" Mom continued questioning, realizing I was very upset about something.

"You know I'd never fight with any of those boys," I quickly responded, with my lips beginning to quiver. "They're the best friends I have!"

Placing her arm around my shoulder, she stated "Well, something seems to be bothering you. I just wish you'd tell me what it was."

Finally breaking down from my mother's relentless prodding, I buried my face in her side and began to cry.

After finally revealing to her what I had just witnessed, Mom quickly stood, cleared a large lump from her throat and said, "Well, maybe we can help."

After going back inside, she removed a gallon jar of milk from the refrigerator, along with a couple packages of butter and several dozen eggs. We then loaded the produce into the car and made a trip to the Mann home. From then on, anytime we had any of these items to spare, Mom would make sure the Mann family got them.

However, just a few years later, Mr. Mann died and the family was moved to a little town about thirty miles away. There, they were given public housing, and began receiving government assistance. This program had been put in place by Franklin D. Roosevelt as part of his New Deal, during Hoover's Great Depression.

Unfortunately, as with many other similar circumstances, this "deal," or whatever it was supposed to be, never quite made it to the Mann family, until after Mr. Mann's unfortunate passing. Looking back on it now, it appears the people in charge of such things, during much of the fifties, were okay with allowing struggling families, through no fault of their own, to suffer every form of humiliation and degradation known to man, other than outright starvation. I assume that falling down and dying along the roadways and in the city streets was just a little more than their delicate sensibilities could justify.

Thank God, when the poverty rate began knocking on the 20% threshold in the early sixties, these programs were strengthened and extended to reach, not only the jobless, but even the working poor…families just like the Mann's prior to the death of their sole income provider.

However, I do realize there's still one powerful entity that's always tried to repeal these vital programs, by creating bogus "straw men" like, "Well Fare Cadillacs" and "Well Fare Queens." I just wish they'd been there, like me, to take a long gander at Mrs. Mann's "gilded throne" pulled up against that steaming laundry pot…or the shiny, new "Cadillac" hidden from view behind that old dilapidated house, while Mr. Mann thumbed his way to work! And I just know they would've seethed with anger at watching those ten "privileged brats" staring with watering mouths as their mother placed the last piece of cornbread onto my plate. If I appear to be making a political statement here…you damn right, I am!

Anyway, I received a letter from Collen about six months after they'd moved away. In it, he told me the family was now living in a house with electricity and indoor plumbing. His mother even had a washing machine…and the kids, a television set! However, he said the thing he was most appreciative of, was no longer having to cram newspapers and rags into the holes in the walls, in order to keep "Father Winter" from making himself at home inside his bedroom!

Now that I've concluded the Mann family's story on a somewhat happy note, I should probably finish telling you about Shep's latest heroic exploit…if I can remember where I was. Oh yeah!

When I noticed that Bess had separated herself far enough from her calf that I could make my way over there and safely pet the little feller, I went to check on Mom. After quickly glancing through the basement door just in time to see her start up the clothes wringer, I knew she'd be busy for a while. So with this expert piece of "reconnoitering" successfully completed, it was now time to put my plan into action.

Without wasting another second, I headed straight for the pasture and slid under the fence. I then began stealthily making my way toward the sleeping calf, while at the same time, keeping a close eye on Bess. When I'd finally gotten within "spitting distance" of my objective, I began to relax a little, while thinking, "Gee, this was easy! What in the world was Dad so worried about?" Then I quickly learned!

The napping calf suddenly awoke and sprung to its feet, while letting loose a frightened, "Blaaaah!" That was all it took to send Bess on an all-out, one-cow stampede straight toward me! For a second or two, I just stood there, frozen in fear. Then, almost like a *Roadrunner and Wiley Coyote* cartoon, my "wheels" began spinning faster than my body was able to move!

Frantically scrambling back across the pasture, I had just about made it to safety, until encountering an obstacle which drastically impeded my progress...the dang drainage ditch from Mom's washing machine. It ran about thirty feet into the pasture, and while looking back over my shoulder at Bess, unfortunately, I stepped dead-smack into the middle of it. That resulted in me turning a mid-air somersault so spectacular, that it would've caused a Romanian gymnast to blush with envy!

However, failing to "nail" the landing, I came down flat on my back! Quickly sitting up, to my horror, I saw that the enraged bovine was only yards away and still charging angrily toward me. I realized it was now too late to get back on my feet and start running again, so I did the only thing I knew to do…scream my guts out for my mother!

But I'm afraid it was too late for that, as well. Old Bess was so close now that I could see blood in her eyes and smell the wild onions on her breath! In other words, my "goose was pretty much cooked" and I was just waiting for the cranberry sauce! That is, until I suddenly caught a flash of sable and white, flying directly over the top of my head.

With a loud thud, Shep met Bess in a mid-air collision so violent that it sent him somersaulting over her entire body, then crashing hard to the ground. This unbelievably heroic act had taken Bess by total surprise, causing the startled cow to "hit the brakes" and begin running back to her calf. But, unfortunately, not before one of her rear hooves had struck the top of my head, knocking me unconscious.

I was just starting to come back around when I heard a strange "ripping" sound. It turned out to be Mom's dress being torn to shreds, as she hurriedly climbed through the five strands of barbed wire and began running toward me. However, my only concern was Shep, and when I saw him lying lifeless on the ground, I jumped to my feet and screamed his name. At about the same time, Mom grabbed me by the arm and attempted to pull me toward the fence. But I wouldn't budge until I saw the brave dog stagger to his feet and groggily shake his head. After finally regaining his senses, Shep turned in the direction of the quickly retreating Bess and began growling.

After seeing that my dog was okay, I ran with Mom to the fence and we climbed back through it. And yes, she ripped her dress again. Fortunately for me, though, her anger was tempered, somewhat, when she noticed the blood streaming down my face. However, I wasn't too awfully concerned about that, because there happened to be another small matter that concerned me quite a bit more.

"Mama, I don't think there's any need in us mentioning anything about this to Daddy," I strongly suggested. "You know how upset he gets over the least little thing!"

Unimpressed, my mother just slowly shook her head while wiping the blood from my face with a piece of her tattered dress, before unambiguously responding, "Boy, you're lucky…but not *that* lucky!"

After Mom had disinfected my wound with a painful splattering of merthiolate, I gave Shep a grateful hug then went inside to let things calm back down. I was hoping this little escapade would quickly be forgotten, then fade quietly into obscurity… but, of course, that wasn't to be. It seems the lady who lived directly across the road from our pasture had witnessed the entire event unfold. And since she just happened to be the main source of information exchange within our little community, it wasn't long before everyone in the general area knew exactly what we did…that there was something very special about that dog!

Run Rabbit Run

I mentioned earlier about my father being rabid about his rabbit hunting…well, not so much the taking of the prey, but the chase involved in it. How well his beagles performed during their weekly seasonal hunts was often how he gauged the hunt's success, not the number of dead rabbits thrown into the back of his brother's pick-up truck, at the end of the day. But of course, the two outcomes usually went hand in hand.

To make sure all of his dogs performed to the best of their abilities, Dad started them in a rigorous training program almost as soon as they were old enough to walk. However, training was only the second phase in producing top quality rabbit dogs. The first was selectively breeding only the adults which demonstrated superior skills in the trailing of the rabbit, and came closest to conforming to the American Kennel Club standards in appearance.

Once those dogs were identified, they became the next in line to be bred, at the appropriate time. Then, if everything went as planned, eight to twelve pups would be whelped from the mating.

Dad then began closely observing the entire litter, attempting to distinguish certain character traits within each individual pup… particularly the qualities he felt would be beneficial in fully developing their hunting prowess. These included; intelligence, courage, a plentiful supply of energy, a natural curiosity, and a certain amount of aggressiveness.

My father also bred his dogs to be on the shorter end of the thirteen to seventeen-inch AKC height standard. Although this meant his beagles would be a little slower afoot than the longer-legged ones, their primary purpose was to keep the rabbit running, not run him into the ground. He also preferred as much white as possible in their tricolor coat pattern, which also included black and brown. This provided them with greater visibility in the thick overgrowth they often hunted in, resulting in a safer hunting environment for them when the rabbits they were often pursuing at close quarters were being shot at.

Dad also had this uncanny ability to distinguish the bark, or "voice," as he referred to it, of each individual dog. This skill was very important in determining which one was leading the chase, or more importantly, picking up the trail after it had been lost by the surprisingly elusive maneuvers of the rabbit. And it was this unusual talent that became very critical when Dad began training his pups. For it allowed him to recognize which ones were the most adept at their calling, thusly insuring that only the best pups would join the pack.

When my father first took up rabbit hunting, after returning home from the war and starting a family, he used wild rabbits that had been caught in traps, or gums, to train his beagles with. However, these rabbits couldn't survive more than a day or two in captivity, and if he didn't use them right away…well, he'd only have a dead rabbit available when he finally found time to release it to his pups. So it was imperative that he use the gum-caught rabbits almost as soon as they were brought to the house.

Accordingly, this was probably the only advantage that working third shift provided my father, because it allowed him more opportunities to use these rabbits before they inevitably succumbed to captivity. He just had to make a long hike through the woods every morning, usually right after getting home from work, to check the traps and gather up any that had been caught. However, when I reached the age of eight or nine, this "job" was turned over to me, but I didn't mind it at all. Besides taking some of the load off the "old man," it presented me with a little early morning excitement.

I remember getting up well before dawn, even on school days, to go check the six or eight gums Dad had set in various locations throughout the woods and fields below our house. Alvin would usually accompany me...well, unless it was raining or severely cold. If that happened to be the case, then he'd just pull the covers up over his head and remain in bed when I would try to rouse him.

I also recall the tremendous excitement every time I'd shine a flashlight on one of them and the lid would be down. The rabbit would always turn toward the rear when I raised the gum on its end and reached inside. So that made it fairly easy to lift them out by their hind legs. I would then place the struggling bunny into the tow sack I always carried with me. But once in a while, I would hear a hissing sound when I approached the gum. This usually meant a possum had been caught. When that happened, I would just pull the lid up and toss it on the ground, then run away.

It wasn't until I got a little older that I became brave enough to just grab them by the tail and yank them out. Even though they would snarl and hiss like little demons, this was only a bluff. They would always choose running over fighting when I turned them loose…if you call their fast escape mode, "running."

By this time, I'd watched my father building the box traps long enough to be able to take on this task, as well, which turned out to be a lot of fun, also. But even more fun was locating the best rabbit trails and feeding locations, near which to set the traps. Even after my father had stopped using these wild rabbits and switched over to the hybrid ones, I continued trapping them just for the fun of it. Of course, I would release the rabbits immediately after catching them.

With the hybrid rabbits becoming Dad's preferred mainstay in training his beagles, it also brought about a different daily regimen for me, also. With him now being able to breed the rabbits in captivity…animals that smelled the same to the pursuing dogs, and eluded them in much the same manner as their wild counterparts…things became much easier for my father, but much harder for me. However, I had no way of knowing just how hard it would get that early spring day, back in 1957!

Shep and I had gone down to the barn one morning, to gather the eggs and feed and water the chickens and rabbits. This was an added chore I'd taken on myself because…well, because Joan and Alvin didn't want to do it, and somebody had to! But I'd be lying if I said I didn't enjoy it, even though it was still my responsibility to bring in firewood for our heating stove, split wood slabs to fill the kitchen wood box, and mow the yard as soon as spring rolled back around. I bet you younger readers are starting to wonder how I found the time to text on my Apple 11, or play video games on my Xbox. You know I'm just messing with you, don't ya?

Once I'd gathered up what eggs had been laid, and placed them in a basket I'd brought with me, I went to the feed bin for the corn-scratch and rabbit pellets. After filling the chicken feeder with the scratch, I walked with Shep around to the rabbit pen with the pellets. Their enclosure consisted of a small shed, holding four cages where the mothers with small babies were kept. The shed was surrounded by a thirty-foot square chicken wire fence which held the other adults, as well as adolescent rabbits.

As I was filling their water containers, I happened to notice that one of the mothers had dug under the fence and, along with her older babies, was frenziedly feasting in a clover patch just a few yards outside the fence. After figuring out what needed to be done, I covered the freshly dug escape route with a couple large rocks, and went inside the barn for a length of bailing twine. I then tied Shep to a small tree, because I knew he'd just be an impediment when I started trying to round all the loose rabbits back up. Once he was secured and out of my way, I opened the gate and attempted to drive the mother and six babies back inside the enclosure.

If you've never "herded" cats, then you wouldn't understand just how difficult an undertaking this turned out to be! But I'm afraid that wasn't the worst of it! With the door being open, several of the other rabbits, who hadn't yet discovered the hole, came hopping out to join their liberated friends.

Finally realizing this wasn't going to be a one-kid job, I went running back to the house in search of assistance. I had only made it about half way there when I saw Alvin and Dean heading in my direction. I promptly yelled for them, then ran back to the rabbit enclosure and went inside the fence. There, I gathered the remaining rabbits and placed them inside the cages. That way, they wouldn't be able to escape while we were trying to catch the ones still "on the lam." In fact, I figured it would probably be a good idea to put the newly captured rabbits inside the cages, also, until they were all apprehended.

After about thirty minutes, with the three of us running around like "Keystone Kops," we finally had all of the wayward bunnies captured and inside the cages. All of the action was closely observed by Shep, of course, who barked excitedly the whole time, from the end of his rope.

Satisfied that the "mission" was successfully accomplished, I untied Shep, picked up my basket of eggs and the four of us went hurrying back to the house. However, in my haste, I'd forgotten one thing. I'd failed to release the rabbits from the cages, and back into the fence. So quickly turning around, I ran back to correct my error, as Alvin and Dean, along with Shep, proceeded on to the house.

That evening, shortly after the family had finished supper, Dad headed out the back door to feed his dogs and milk Old Bess. However, not long afterward, he unexpectedly walked back through the door…but this time, with fire in his eyes!

"You! Come with me!" he demanded, while angrily pointing his finger right in my face.

Mom, who was sitting next to me watching TV, looked up at him with an intense look of concern, and promptly asked, "What in the world is wrong?"

But Dad didn't volunteer any type of explanation for his odd behavior. He just continued staring coldly at me as I tentatively walked to where he was standing. After sternly nudging me out the back door and down the steps, he then took the lead as we headed straight for the barn.

As soon as we rounded the rear corner, Dad stopped dead in his tracks and pointed toward the rabbit pen. I walked on by him, and before even getting half way there, a chilling sight filled my eyes. Scattered throughout the enclosure, were rabbits lying in all sorts of contorted positions. But what was even more chilling, every single one of them appeared stone-cold dead.

Stunned, I simply turned back toward Dad and limply shrugged my shoulders while raising both my hands, to show him that I had no explanation for what had taken place there.

After somehow regathering my wits about me, I finally stammered, "I…I don't know what happened! They were all just fine this morning."

"Well, I'll tell you exactly what happened!" Dad scowled, pointing at Shep who was standing at my feet. "Look at his mouth!"

Dropping to my knees, I took Shep's head in my hands and, to my utter shock and dismay, discovered that the hair around his mouth was completely bloodstained…and most telling of all, there was rabbit fur stuck to the blood.

"Shep what did you do? You know you're not supposed to hurt the rabbits!" I screamed at him, as he dropped his tail and lowered his head, suddenly realizing he had done something to displease me.

"I think I know why he did it!" I exclaimed, jumping back to my feet and confronting Dad. "One of the mama rabbits dug under the fence…and she and her babies were out when I came to feed and water them this morning!"

Then, quickly walking over to where I had covered the hole with rocks, I pointed to it and said, "See…this is where it was.

Alvin, Dean and me caught 'em all, and put 'em back in the fence. Then I put…"

Suddenly stopping in mid-sentence, I noticed that the rocks had been pushed aside and the hole dug even deeper and wider.

Seething with anger, and not the least bit swayed by my partial explanation, Dad quickly cut me off with, "Those rabbits were killed inside the fence, not outside it…and now you see how he got in!"

He then turned around and began walking quickly back toward the house. Terrified of what he might do to my dog, I took off running to catch up. After falling in behind Dad, I tried hard to match him stride for stride while, at the same time, attempting to complete my explanation of what I thought had taken place… and why.

"I tied Shep to a tree while we were running the rabbits down and putting them in the cages, inside the shed. Shep must've thought we were catching them for food or something, since he never saw any of them again. I didn't let them back inside the fence until after Shep had already gone back to the house with Alvin and Dean. I reckon he came back down while we were eating supper, and saw that there were still rabbits that hadn't been caught. So, I guess he decided to go inside the fence and finish the job," I reasoned, then waited for a response from Dad. But to my horror and dread, his response turned out to be the last thing I wanted to hear.

"That dumb story might get you off the hook…but not that damn dog!" he roared while swiftly climbing the back steps.

When Dad entered the house and walked into the rear bedroom, I began pleading with him, "If somebody has to be punished, then it oughta be me! Because it was my fault for letting it happen. But please don't whip Shep!"

Suddenly, cold chills went racing up and down my spine, when Dad ignored my pleas and, instead, reached for the gun rack on the wall. After taking down his old twelve-gauge double barrel, he turned to me and replied, "Who said anything about whipping him?"

About this time, Mom ran into the room to see what was going on. I looked up at her and it was all I could do to get the words out of my mouth when I screamed, "Mama, don't let him!"

"Long Crawley, you'd better come to your senses, before you do something really stupid!" she warned.

Still fuming with anger and completely undeterred by Mom's warning, Dad broke the barrels down and threw a shell into one of the chambers. He then walked back out onto the porch and removed one of the dog leashes from its hook on the wall. With me crying and Mom still swearing at him, Dad opened the back door and started down the steps.

Shep, who was standing at the bottom of them, just looked curiously up at me when Dad looped it around his neck. Not knowing anything more I could do, I just looked mournfully back at him. But when my still livid father began leading him back down to the barn, I ran for the door. However, Mom not wanting me anywhere near my enraged father while he was carrying a loaded gun, caught my arm just as I reached the top step, and starting pulling me back inside. Seeing her mother straining to get me back through the door, Joan came running to her aid and grabbed my other arm.

"Noooooo!" I screamed as loud as I could, then turned and began sobbing into Mom's dress, as she held on to me, tightly.

When Dad reached the barn and started around behind it

with my dog, Mom yelled out one last threat, "Long Crawley, if you do that…then keep on walking! Don't you even bother coming back here!"

"Surely, that'll stop him," I thought, as a slight glimmer of hope began making its way into my head. However, that glimmer was suddenly extinguished when a loud "boom!" came echoing back to the house.

I immediately fell limp, then began pulling violently against Mom and Joan's grip, until I was finally free. I then began frantically sprinting for the barn. But just as I got there, Dad came walking from behind it, still carrying the shotgun…with one of the barrels still smoking. He was still holding one end of the leash, with Shep still attached to the other…and still wagging his tail!

Sobbing, I dropped to my knees and threw my arms around Shep's neck. Without any sign of regard or sympathy for my feelings, Dad simply handed me the leash, along with the admonishment, "If he ever pulls a stunt like that again, I will shoot him!"

Finally realizing the whole charade had been meant as punishment for me…I guess, for not keeping a tighter rein on my dog, thus allowing what had happened…I glared angrily up at him, and was just about to say something that would've gotten me into a lot more trouble, when Mom finally arrived on the scene and said it for me.

"Damn you, Long Crawley! Just damn you!" she snarled disgustedly at him, while he just smiled sheepishly back.

If some of you readers are beginning to suspect this wasn't the "Cleaver" family…well, you're absolutely right!

Angel and Serpent

Not too long after this little "hare-raising" affair had concluded and been put to rest, things finally began to settle back down. There happened to be two mother rabbits with small babies in a couple of the cages, so Shep was unable to get to them. And being that those little critters propagate faster than Catholics on Viagra, the rabbit pen was soon bouncing with bunnies, once again. I just had to spend several hours of hard labor placing large rocks around the fence perimeter, to make sure this fiasco was never repeated.

However, it was probably a lot of unnecessary work and effort on my part. I think Shep understood what he did was wrong, by just how upset I became when confronting him about it. Now don't get me wrong. I'm not, in any way, suggesting that he understood, word for word, what I was saying to him. But Shep did have this uncanny ability to put two and two together to get four. And no, the dog couldn't do arithmetic. I'm just using that as an analogy.

Anyway, like I said, after this most recent entry in *The Crawley Family Chronicles,* things soon returned to normal around our house. Now, you have to keep in mind, "normal" for me, back then, was always relative…and it usually only lasted a short time. But before I open this next "can of worms," I should probably fill you in on what was taking place in my life, immediately prior.

I was still very much involved with my exercise program, along with Dad. But instead of the original morning time slot, we had switched to evenings because of me starting school. I was also still making my once-a-month visits to the physical therapy clinic in Morganton, but on Saturdays instead of weekdays, as had been the case.

Other than being informed that my respiratory system was functioning adequately, the examination turned out to be pretty disturbing during my September, 1957 visit. It seems the doctors were concerned that my skeletal growth appeared to be outpacing my muscular development. If this problem continued, it would result in my shoulders stooping even more, and my ribs pressing in on my weakened diaphragm. This would cause me difficulty in breathing, with the only solution being the dreaded, aforementioned back brace.

Although I no longer had to worry about being "fitted" with an iron lung, this latest development was still pretty traumatic for me. Now, don't think for a second I'm seeking sympathy or pity, because I realize many of you had your own problems growing up, as did most kids. However, fretting over constantly being misunderstood, managing peer pressure, or not relating well to others don't count…and neither does freaking out over your latest acne breakout, and fretting over whether or not it'll clear up in time for the senior prom. Heck, all of that stuff would've just been "chump change" compared to what was keeping me up at night!

Anyhow, receiving this latest round of bad news caused me to lie awake at night thinking about having to run and play with that thing on, and being teased by the other kids when I did. And no one can be crueler to kids, than other kids. I'm afraid I had to learn that hard lesson while only in the second grade, and this is how it came about:

Shortly after the beginning of that school year, I saw one of the boys I had shared the hospital ward in Asheville with. Oh, he wasn't hard to recognize, at all! And how could he be, with him limping along well back of the line, as his class made their way to the cafeteria? The fact that he wore braces on both legs, and kept his swiveled right arm pulled tightly against his side, must've been high humor to several other boys. For they were walking back there with him, but only to mock his "waddling" gate.

I immediately began wishing that he and I had been put in the same classroom. At least, that way, he would've had a friend. Someone who understood what he was going through, someone to help him up and down steps when he was carrying a load of books…and someone to punch those little "bastages" right in the mouth!

But the way it was, being totally isolated from his peers because of his physical disabilities, the poor boy must've felt entirely alone, and completely different from everyone else. And witnessing this taking place on a daily basis, began having a detrimental effect on my mental wellbeing, as well.

In addition to feeling pity for the poor kid, I'm almost ashamed to admit it, but I began worrying even more about my own physical problems. If kids would do that to him, then they'd do the same to me, if I were forced to wear a back brace. I could just imagine them teasing and laughing at me when I tried to play, while being held rigid by that thing…or even sitting at my desk, stiff and upright, like a dime store mannequin!

If all of that wasn't bad enough, I also began experiencing a tremendous feeling of guilt. After all, I was the only boy in that hospital ward to walk out of there without having to be fitted with at least one leg brace. All the times before when I would think about it, I just felt lucky…if you consider what I was dealing with, "lucky." But, at least, I did have hope. That little kid had none. And every time I watched him leave his classroom with the other kids, and fall farther and farther behind them, I knew he had to feel like the loneliest kid in the world. Because that's exactly how I felt, until Shep came along.

With all of these thoughts constantly on my mind, I started to become more and more withdrawn from everyone, or anything outside the little protective "bubble" I had built around me. It came to a head one morning at school, just as class was about to begin. My teacher was calling the roll and when she got to my name, I didn't hear her because of the inattentive state I had taken refuge in.

"Jerry, are you going to join the rest of the class this morning?" I finally heard her say…and then the sound of laughter all around me.

My only response was to drop my head on my desk and just sit there, motionless. With that, she walked over to me and asked, "Are you not feeling well today?" To which, I just shrugged my shoulders.

Becoming even more perplexed, she then asked, "Do you have a headache…or maybe an upset stomach?" To which I simply shook my head.

When my teacher suddenly became quiet, and just stood over me…and I knew the other students were all staring at me…I just couldn't take anymore and began to sob.

Upon seeing this, she leaned over and softly whispered, "Jerry, would you like to go to the nurse's station and lie down?"

After finally being offered a way out of this embarrassing predicament, I quickly nodded, "yes."

When I stood and stepped away from my desk, she placed her hand on my shoulder and began escorting me out of the classroom and down the hall to a room next to the principal's office. After walking through the door, my teacher motioned to one of the small cots in the room, and directed me to go lie down. She then proceeded over to the desk and began conversing with the nurse. I closely observed them as they whispered back and forth to one another, while glancing over at me from time to time. When my teacher finally left the room, the nurse walked over to my bed.

"So you're having a bad day?" she correctly assumed.

When I just nodded, she smiled and said, "I believe you have an older sister in the elementary building, don't you?"

After again nodding to the nurse, she just looked at me for several seconds, then suggested, "I bet if she were to come down here and sit with you for a little while, you'd start feeling much better."

This time, I spoke up and said, "Yeah, I think I would, too." And when I saw my sister's familiar face, I knew the nurse had made the right call!

"They told me you weren't feeling so good this morning," Joan stated, after walking over and sitting down in a chair next to the bed.

"I don't know what's wrong with me," I lied. "I just feel real sad today...and want to go home."

Hearing this, my sister looked curiously at me for several seconds, then said, "You never got homesick one single time last year...and this year, you're a big second-grader. So you just need to try to snap out of it, and start thinking happy thoughts. Then everything will be okay!"

"I can't think of any happy thoughts," I replied.

"Oh, is that right?" she replied. "Just who do you think's going to be waiting beside the road when you get off the bus this afternoon?"

That was all Joan needed to say to cheer me right up! And when the old bus crested the final hill, before our front yard came into view, there sat Shep exactly where Joan said he'd be!

Alvin got off first and ran right by the dog, without Shep even looking up at him. Then came Joan, and he wagged his tail as she gave him a pat on the head then proceeded on to the house. But when Shep saw me step out and begin running across the road, he began prancing excitedly from side to side, while furiously wagging his tail. And when I leapt across the ditch and entered the yard, he almost knocked me to the ground, while jumping up to lick my face. At that very moment, everything became right with the world and all of my troubles were quickly swept aside.

However, misfortune always seemed to be following close on my heels, and not long afterward, it caught up with me again. I had just gotten home from school on a really gorgeous, early October, Friday afternoon. I knew it would be about an hour until Mom had supper ready, and since it was the start of the weekend, I didn't have any homework that needed doing, right then. So I decided to take advantage of the beautiful fall weather, with a quick romp in the woods.

The sweltering heat of summer had long since morphed into the more pleasant temperatures of September, and was now being cooled even further by the shorter daylight periods of early autumn, my favorite time of year. As we made our way past the barn and entered the woods below it, I marveled at how the once radiantly green hardwood canopy was starting to transition into even more vibrant hues of red, orange and yellows. I also took notice of the numerous grey squirrels who were busy gathering up the bountiful harvest of acorns and hickory nuts that were falling profusely to the ground.

Shep noticed them, too…and went chasing after one that had been peeling the scales off of a ripened pine cone. I continued on down the trail, and was just about to enter a small, grassy meadow when he caught back up with me. There, the path narrowed, and was bordered on both sides by tall broom grass. Suddenly, I came to an abrupt stop when I heard a high-pitched, bussing sound coming from somewhere near my feet. At first, I thought it was a cicada…then quickly realized that they should've been long gone by then. When I started to take another step, the buzzing sound became even more threatening and sinister. So I just remained frozen in my tracks, afraid to move.

About this time, Shep came bounding past me, knocking me to the opposite side of the trail from where the strange sound was coming. Paralyzed with fear, I could only watch as the brave dog lunged into the thick grass, then began yelping with pain. When it seemed the situation couldn't get any more terrifying, he suddenly came backing out of the grass…with a large snake clasped firmly between his jaws.

Still unable to move, I began to question if what I was witnessing was actually taking place. It reminded me of one of those weird dreams I had from time to time. You know, where something scary is chasing you, and no matter how hard you try, you just can't seem to get your feet to cooperate? However, the unimaginable scene became very real when the snake struck Shep on the nose again, causing him to let out another painful yelp. Becoming enraged, I suddenly forgot my fear and sprang into action.

Grabbing the snake by the tail, I tried to pull it from Shep's mouth…and finally did! However, it was only half of the snake, but that turned out to be enough. The other half that Shep was still holding, coiled itself up into a ball, which he flung angrily to the ground. He then began shaking his head violently, in an attempt to remove the painful burning sensation from his face. When that failed, he dropped to his belly and began pulling at his snout with both paws.

Incognizant of what I had just done, I was suddenly jolted back to my senses when I felt something wiggling around in my hands. In utter panic, I threw the half snake as far away from me as I could! Then, as soon as I was able to stop screaming, I commenced running back up the trail as fast as my legs would carry me.

Once I had gotten within sight of the house, I began yelling for Dad. Unfortunately, my oxygen-starved lungs were unable to take in enough air for me to get any sound to come out. However, Dad just happened to be sitting on the back steps when I finally arrived there. Seeing him, I came to a stop and managed to catch my breath just long enough to yell, "Shep got bit by a snake!"

The stricken dog, who had been following at my heels,

suddenly dropped to the ground and, once again, began pawing at his face. Seeing this, Dad quickly got to his feet and ran over to Shep. While rubbing his thumb across several small puncture wounds that were still oozing blood, he stated rather stoically, "Yeah, he's been snake bit, all right," finally confirming what I already knew.

"What can we do for him?" I immediately asked.

My father just shook his head and bluntly replied, "Not much of anything."

"There's got to be *something* that can be done for him!" I shouted.

"Ah…I don't think it's all that bad," Dad tried to assure me. "My beagles git bit by copperheads all the time. It hurts purty bad…and they'll swell up for a couple days…but they always seem to git over it, without anything havin' to be done for'em."

"Do copperheads make a weird buzzing sound before they bite?" I quickly asked, hoping for something positive from him.

"Well, no…that sounds more like a timber rattler!" Dad replied. "They're ornery and mean this time of year…and still out tryin' to catch 'em a squirrel or two, before dennin' up for the winter. If that's what bit him…well, that's a whole different story!"

Trying hard to hold back the tears that were beginning to form in my eyes, I led Shep around to the front porch, where he climbed the steps and slumped down on his mat.

As he lay on his side, taking rapid, shallow breaths, Dad contemplatively ran his hand across his mouth, then said, "Well, maybe there is something that might help him...a little."

He then turned to Mom, who had just stepped out onto the front porch, and said, "Sue, how 'bout roundin' up one of your old dish pans, and fill it about half full of ice water."

As she started back into the house, with Joan close on her heels, Dad added, "Oh…and an old towel, too."

Once the pan of ice water was readied and sitting next to him, Dad dipped the towel in it, wrung most of the water back out, then placed it around Shep's rapidly swelling head.

All this is gonna do, is help keep the swellin' down," he explained. "And it might help a little with the pain, too. But the rest will be purty much up to the dog…and you."

With that, Dad handed the towel over to me, then opened the front door and walked inside the house."

For the remainder of the evening, and up into the night, I kept a freshly dipped towel on Shep's severely swollen head. While I was doing this, Mom continued adding fresh ice to the water, as quickly as she was able to freeze it. On her final delivery of the evening, she considerately offered, "Why don't you let me handle that for a while, so you can go eat your supper?"

I just looked up at her with a mournful expression and said, "I'm not hungry, Mama…and I don't think I could eat anything, even if I was."

"Well, okay then. I'll give you one more hour, then you have to come inside and get ready for bed," she instructed, then turned and walked back through the door.

When that hour was finally up, Mom came back out and knelt down beside me.

"You know, that dog's not taken his eyes off you the whole time he's been laying there," she mused, while gently stroking the top of Shep's head. "It's almost as though he knows he can't leave you, so he just keeps fightin' to stay alive."

Then, struggling to keep her emotions in check, Mom quickly stood, cleared her throat and said, "Okay, young man, time to go to bed."

Before standing up myself, I leaned over and gave Shep a tender hug, which he returned by weakly wagging his tail.

But before we made it to the door, Dad came out it carrying one of his old army blankets, which he spread over the shivering dog.

"This is what we did for shot-up soldiers, while waitin' on a stretcher. It helped 'em retain their body heat, so they wouldn't go into shock," he informed Mom and me.

"Do you think he'll make it through this?" I asked, trying to pry just a small measure of hope from my father, so I'd be able to leave Shep's side not feeling quite so guilty. After all, if I hadn't decided to take that jaunt in the woods, my best friend wouldn't be lying there in such pain. But instead, I was left totally demoralized by his terse reply.

"I wouldn't get my hopes up too high," he matter-of-factly stated, before opening the front door and walking back inside.

I then quickly looked up at my mother, hoping I might get that much-needed solace from her…and she didn't disappoint!

Placing an arm around my shoulder, she said, "It'll be tough, but I believe Shep's going to pull through this, somehow. I've witnessed too many amazing things from that dog, in the short time he's been here, to think that God's done with him, already."

Those were just the words I needed to hear...but Mama always had a way of saying things like that. And how I hoped they were true, as I followed her into the house, then went to my bedroom.

That night, I prayed harder than I ever had before, then surrendered to a troubled and fitful sleep. Waking up just a couple hours later, I slipped back into my clothes and tip-toed out onto the porch. Shep's breathing was still labored, and every so often he'd softly moan, as if in severe pain…which I'm sure he was. After gently stroking his neck, I lifted one end of the blanket and slid under it. If the poor dog had to endure something so painful because of me, then I was going to share some of the suffering with him.

I was finally roused from my uncomfortable and chilly repose by Dad's voice and daylight.

"Well, at least he's still alive. But from the looks of him, it's hard to tell if that's good or bad!" he discouragingly informed me.

Glancing over at Shep, after quickly sitting up and rubbing my eyes, I was extremely shocked at what I saw. Along with his head, the dog's tongue was swollen to twice its normal size. So much so, in fact, that he was now unable to close his mouth. And even more disheartening, he was still lying in the same position, and his breathing remained very shallow and strained.

Struggling to hold back my tears, I reached over and gently rubbed the side of Shep's bloated face. As soon as he felt my hand, he rolled his eyes in my direction and made a feeble attempt to wag his tail.

"Daddy, there's got to be something more we can do for him!" I frustratingly cajoled my father. "What we've been doing, don't seem to be working worth a darn!"

"Like I said, the dog's still alive, ain't he?" he gruffly replied. "So it's gotta be helpin' him some. Now, go on in the house and eat your breakfast, so you can git back to work."

All day long, Dad and I took turns soaking a towel in the freezing water and wrapping it around Shep's head. While this was going on, Mom continued making ice in whatever vessel she could find that would hold water. When darkness finally fell on that long Saturday, we were all thoroughly exhausted and began preparing for bed a little earlier than usual. We needed to be up fairly early the following morning to attend church…well, except for Dad. For some reason I never quite understood, he failed to adopt that particular weekly "ritual."

At the end of the day, Shep was still too weak to change positions on his mat, and was still struggling to take oxygen into his lungs, one forced breath at a time. When I knelt down next to him one final time before going inside, he again rolled his sad, brown eyes my way and weakly raised his tail, before dropping it back to the floor. Not knowing if he'd still be with me when I awoke the following morning, I leaned over and kissed his forehead, then left him alone to battle through another torturous night.

As soon as the morning light broke through my bedroom window, I was up pulling on my trousers. However, before I could open the front door and run out onto the porch, Mom stopped me in my tracks with, "Hey, not so fast, young man! You have to eat breakfast before going out there."

I don't believe it was so much a matter of Mom being overly concerned about my daily nutritional intake, as it was what I might see when I walked out that door. I'm sure she wanted Dad to go out there first. Then, he could inform me of Shep's condition.

When he finally walked through the kitchen and toward the front door, Dad glanced over at me as I was rearranging the food on my plate with my fork. I was just too worried about the bad news I might receive to eat. After a couple minutes, he stepped back inside with an expression on his face that failed to displace any of that worry.

"Well, I still don't know if he's gonna make it or not. But one thing's for damn sure…that dog's a fighter!" he declared, allowing me to finally exhale.

Quickly looking over at Mom, I asked, "Can I?"

"Oh…go ahead," was all it took for me to slide under the table and go running for the front door.

When I sat down next to Shep and began tenderly petting him, he once again acknowledged my presence by rolling his eyes in my direction, along with a single wag of his tail. Then, with tears streaming from eyes, I began talking to him.

"Buddy, I've been praying real hard for God to make you better, but it doesn't look like that's working out so good. So I'm gonna ask someone a whole lot closer to him than me, to pray for you, too. Maybe that'll be enough, I don't know…but I have to try something different. And you'll have to try hard for me, too," I told him, before breaking down and weeping, inconsolably.

Several minutes passed before I was able to collect myself enough to finish saying to Shep what I'd started telling him. When I had, I wiped my eyes with my fingers and said to him, "I have to leave you for a little while, to go to church. But before I leave there, I'm gonna have a little talk with Preacher McKinney. He's a real good man, and if anybody can get through to God for us, it'll be him."

I then gave Shep one final pat on the head, then went back inside to get ready for church.

The church we attended was Bethel Methodist, a small, but stately, brick cathedral which ministered to a congregation of about one hundred…on a good day. It was located about a half mile south of our house…close enough that I could walk back home after services were over, if Mom happened to be tied up with a meeting or something.

The pastor was Reverend William McKinney, who had been

born and raised in the nearby mountains, and was very well regarded by nearly all of the parishioners. Our church was one of three others in the diocese, so Pastor McKinney could only conduct services at two of them on a given Sunday. Not only were we on his schedule that day, but the service would also be the later one, allowing me the time I needed to discuss my problem with him.

When Preacher McKinney concluded his sermon, he closed the Bible on his lectern, then bowed his head for the final prayer. When he finished, the congregation began singing a hymn as the pastor walked to the door. There, he shook hands with each departing attendee, after the song had ended. However, when my family stood to leave, I remained seated until all of the pews were empty, then took my turn.

"Well Butch, you're usually the first one out the door!" Preacher McKinney exclaimed. "Don't tell me you fell asleep again?"

"No, Preacher McKinney," I responded, staring shyly down at my shoe laces. "It was just that I have a big favor to ask of you… and wanted to do it alone."

"Well certainly!" he replied, kneeling down on one knee so we could be a little more discreet.

When tears suddenly began streaming down my cheeks, the preacher's smile was quickly replaced by a look of compassion and concern.

"Shep got snake bit Friday evening, and I don't think he's gonna make it!" I finally blurted out. "I've been praying real hard for him, but it doesn't seemed to have done him any good."

"Whoa…hold on just a second," Preacher McKinney requested, while gently placing a hand on my shoulder. He then reached in his coat pocket for a handkerchief, for me to dry my eyes with.

"Shep? That's not one of Long's beagles, is it?" he asked, as he had gone hunting with Dad and Uncle Pat on a number of occasions.

Suddenly remembering that Shep and the preacher had never met, I quickly clarified my statement.

"Oh no, Preacher. Shep is *my* dog…and the best friend I have in the whole world!" I told him.

"Oh…I understand," Preacher McKinney replied. "So I take it, you want me to pray for Shep, also?"

"If you would. I mean…you know God a whole lot better than I do…and he may be able to hear your prayers better than he can hear mine," I explained.

Pastor McKinney just smiled and replied, "God knows all of us equally, Butch…and I'm certain he hears your prayers just fine. But sometimes one more can make a big difference. Especially, when you request it from someone, because it shows him that you haven't lost faith. So, I'll tell you what I'll do. Before I leave here today, I'll go back to the altar, get down on my knees and say the best prayer I have in me, for Shep's recovery. But you'll need to do a little something for me, in return. Oh…and for God, too!"

"I'll do anything, Preacher McKinney…if it'll help Shep," I assured him.

"Okay Butch, we've got a deal, then," the pastor replied, once again shaking my hand. "I want you to try to talk your dad into attending the church service, when I'm back here in two weeks."

I tried hard to hide the grimace that inadvertently formed on my face from the well-intended minister's request, but I'm sure he noticed it. And the reason I grimaced was because I knew talking my father into attending church services would be about as hopeless as trying to locate a *Second* Baptist Church.

However, I assured Preacher McKinney I would give it my best shot…then loudly blew my dripping nose on the handkerchief he had loaned me, before offering it back to him.

"Uh…why don't you just hold on to that?" he said, before turning and walking back into the church sanctuary.

When we arrived back home, the first thing I noticed, as Mom pulled into our driveway, was Dad leaning over Shep. Not knowing what to expect, I climbed out of the car somewhat apprehensively, and slowly approached them. After noticing that my dog was still breathing, I released an audible sigh, then asked, "What are you doing now?"

"I thought I'd try something a little different today," Dad answered. "Up until now, we've been usin' cold water to help keep the swellin' down. But now, I've switched to hot water, with a few special ingredients mixed in, to draw out some of the poison and infection."

Sitting down next to Shep, I leaned over and peered into the steaming pan of hot water, and immediately felt a stinging sensation running up my nostrils.

Quickly jerking my head away, I asked, "What in the world did you put in there?"

"Oh, it's just a disinfectin' concoction we used in the Medical Corps. If a wounded soldier was left out in the field for a while, and his wounds got infected, this is what we treated him with 'til we could get him to a field hospital, or on a boat," he replied. "It's mainly Epsom salt, apple vinegar and mustard poultice….oh, and a pint of white liquor I had stashed away in the basement for special occasions. Of course, we never seemed to have any of that still layin' around, when we needed it for medical purposes!"

When Dad revealed that last "special" ingredient, he looked up at Mom with a wry grin plastered across his face. Which she responded to by simply picking up the empty Mason jar, taking a quick whiff, and sitting it back down while disgustedly shaking her head. She then opened the front door and stepped inside… but not before dryly commenting, "He must care a lot more about that dog than he's been lettin' on!"

Dad just chuckled a little at Mom's remark, then showed me something else he was doing for Shep. Next to the disinfectant pan was a smaller bowl filled with fresh water. And lying next to it was a large syringe, which he used for administering liquid medicines to his beagles.

"Shep ain't been able to stand on his feet to drink. And even if he could, his tongue is swelled up so big that he can't lap up the water. So I've been usin' this here syringe to force it down his throat," he explained, while demonstrating the process to me.

"I hadn't even thought about that," I said. "I guess he was pretty thirsty!"

"He don't seem to be able to git enough of it!" Dad replied. "He's swallered down every drop I've give him, and still seems to want more! Now, go on in the house and change your clothes. Then, after dinner, you can take over doin' this," Dad instructed me.

For the remainder of the day, I stayed busy wrapping Shep's head with towels soaked in Dad's newly concocted "elixir." And every couple hours, I would give him a syringe full of cold water, which he eagerly gulped down. My diligent nursing was finally rewarded when I returned to Shep's side one final time before going to bed. To my delight, I found him lying on his opposite side…and no one had helped him!

The next morning, I realized it would be hopeless, as well as totally futile, to ask Mom if I could skip school that day, and continue treating Shep…but I did, anyway.

"Absolutely not, young man!" came her expected reply. But she assured me my dog would be in capable hands, until I returned home.

Before walking down to the bus line, I gave Shep a pat on the head and told him I'd be home in a little while. When he strained to lift his head, then feebly wagged his tail, I felt a little less guilty about leaving him.

Although I physically attended school that day, I'm afraid I failed to make the trip mentally. Most of the day, my eyes remained transfixed on the big clock on the wall, while only paying scant attention to my teacher. When the hands finally came to rest on three-twenty (yes, I'd finally learned how to decipher the son-of-a-gun by then) and the bell began ringing, I quickly headed for the doors and straight to the bus line! And when I finally arrived back home, I received the shock of my young life. For sitting in his usual spot, as though the whole ordeal had only been a really bad dream, was Shep!

With tears welling up in my eyes, I almost fell down the bus steps, trying to get off as fast as I could and run to him. As soon as he saw me crossing the road, Shep stood on wobbly legs and began furiously wagging his tail. And I almost fell again, as I excitedly leapt across the ditch to enter our yard, and finally embrace him.

"I've never seen anything like it in my life!" Mom said, walking down to where I was holding tightly onto my beloved dog. "About ten minutes before it was time for the bus to get here, he just got up off of his mat and stumbled down the steps. Then, started slowly making his way across the yard, toward the road, just barely able to walk. I didn't think he was going to make it, but somehow he did!"

That evening, after getting out of bed, Dad walked out onto the front porch to check on Shep. When he saw him sitting upright, he exclaimed, "Well, I'll be damned! I didn't give that dog a beggar's chance of pullin' out of this!"

Then, as he knelt down to take a closer look at him, he kind of mumbled to himself, "Don't know if it was a miracle…or my expert doctorin'."

Before offering up my own opinion, I suddenly remembered the pastor's request and casually mentioned to Dad, "I had a talk with Preacher McKinney before leaving church, yesterday. He wanted to know if there was any chance of you attending services, when he's back at our church in two weeks."

Dad just chuckled as got back on his feet and began walking toward the front door. Then, before opening it, he turned to me and said, "Tell Bill there's two chances, slim and none. And "ol' Slim's" done rode out of town!"

With that, I was reluctantly forced to accept the harsh reality that Shep's amazing recovery was more likely the result of Dad's "expert doctoring." Because miracles just weren't happening.

The Hanging Tree

I'm sure you're well aware by now that my family wasn't able to acquire a television set until the summer of 1955, when I was six years old. With that in mind, let me point out that it seemed we were always one of the last households, among our circle of family and friends, to acquire many of these modern technologies, which were quickly becoming common place in the early '50's.

It's still difficult to imagine when I think back on it, but Mom still cooked on a wood-burning stove throughout all of that decade, and a year or two into the next. I even recall some of our friends and relatives, who owned electric stoves, coming over to eat with us and commenting about how much better the food tasted when cooked that way. However, I just rolled my eyes when I would hear that kind of talk, and think, "Yeah, let 'em chop that hard oak wood, using Dad's old dull axe for a couple hours, and it'll taste even better!"

Anyway, getting back to the point I was trying to make, I don't believe our belated acquisition of these modern technologies was entirely due to us being poor, or even my father being tight with his money, although he could squeeze a nickel until it screamed. But for some reason, other families that weren't any better off, financially, than we were, seemed to be acquiring these things several years before we were able to.

What I do believe it was, though, was Dad's stubborn resistance to change. In other words, I think he had become so entrenched and comfortable in his way of living and doing things, it was all but impossible for him to adapt to different or more modern methods. I didn't come to this realization until later in life, when it suddenly dawned on me that I had inherited much of this same tendency.

The first clue I had of this, was when I was in my late twenties. I had traveled out of town for a weekend softball tournament, and was sharing a room with three of my team mates. While the other guys were shaving that first morning, using canned foam and plastic throw-a-way razors, I'm afraid I was brushing on soap from out of a shaving mug, then scraping it off with a metal safety razor. I didn't even realize how behind-the-times this was, until one of the guys began kidding me about it.

"Hey, Crawley…was the straight razor and leather strap just a little too much for your toiletry kit?" I believe was how the first joke went. But that's the way my old man had always done it, so it was still good enough for me!

And many years later when the cell phone became an essential, never-to-be-without possession, I would hang on to my old, outdated one until I broke it, or it just stopped working, even though I could get a new, up-to-date phone, free of charge, through a work program my wife was eligible for. I guess the reason for this was, I had become comfortable with the old one, and really didn't want to have to learn the different functions a new phone would require.

Even to this day, I drive a thirty-five year old pick-up truck that I've had the engine replaced in once, the interior redone twice and the body painted three times, simply because I've grown attached to it. So, as you're probably starting to understand by now, this little personality quirk which I shared with my father wasn't so much out of necessity, but more due to an acquired comfort level and, to a lesser degree, sentimentality.

However, for some reason that I'm presently unable to recall, we seemed to be living pretty "high on the hog" that particular summer. Besides the TV, Dad also purchased a brand new '56 Chevrolet Bel Air, later that autumn. It replaced the old, beat up '50 Chevrolet that had replaced the old, dilapidated 46 Chevrolet that had brought me home from the orthopedic hospital. Are any of you starting to suspect that my dad may have been a Chevy fan?

But anyhow, it sure felt good not to have to slump down in the back seat, whenever we happened to pass by some of my schoolmates who weren't familiar with the latest old "clunker" my family owned! However, what was even neater about obtaining the new car, was that my mother was finally motivated to learn to drive…being that this one had an automatic transmission.

What was so neat about that, you ask? Well, it meant that we kids got to go to a lot more places, and do a lot more fun stuff. And that was a pretty big deal for three little "hayseeds" that hardly ever got off the farm!

However, as it turned out, the new Emerson TV had an even greater impact on my life than the new car. Now, who would've imagined that? No longer was our old radio constantly pumping out the country music that had become the "sound track" for my life. If you're a little confused about that statement, watch the old movie classic, *The Last Picture Show,* sometime and maybe it'll clear it up for you. In it, Hank Williams songs are continually being played in the background, through either a car radio, a home radio or a jukebox. I guess that's why it's always been one of my favorite motion pictures. And, evidently, that old radio really had a strong influence on my young life because, even to this day, in the corner of my mind stands a jukebox. Gosh, wouldn't that make a great country song lyric? Oh, wait! (Remember what I said…even if it's bad!)

Also, with having our very own television, I no longer had to go across the road to watch my paternal grandmother's. I'm sure she was relieved, too. Because she would always turn it to something she knew I wouldn't like…maybe a news program, or a football game…just to get me to go home. You know, now that I think about it, that's probably the main reason we were never very close. But that's okay, I'm over it now.

TV viewing quickly became my favorite pastime, and the program I looked forward to most, as did the rest of the family, was *The Adventures of Lassie*. Well…unless, of course, there happened to be a "cowboy show" on at the same time slot. Would you believe I still have a soft spot for those things?

The program aired on Sunday evenings, and for all of you "old timers" who still remember it, I'm referring to the original series…the one which featured *Jeff* as the main human character. He was without a father, for some reason unspecified by the show's writers, and, thusly, lived with only his mother and grandfather. In the later one, the character, *Timmy*, comprised this same role. But unlike Jeff, he enjoyed a more typical family life, with both a mother *and* father. However, he just seemed like too much of a "dweeb" to capture enough of my interest.

Anyway, in the TV episodes I'm referring to, Lassie was always performing spectacular deeds and making amazing rescues of Jeff. And even though I was still a young child, I realized this was only Hollywood fantasy, and these types of heroics, by an animal, would never occur in real life.

Now, I know what you're probably thinking, *but*...even though Shep had saved me from Old Bess, and the snake, and even the "unmounted headless horseman" in our back yard, those were actual physical threats that he could see, hear and smell. Therefore, his only recourse was to physically engage them, just as many loyal dogs would've done. However, most of the ordeals involving Jeff were more abstract in nature than the ones Shep had encountered with me...situations that a mere dog wouldn't, necessarily, consider a threat. Yet, somehow, Lassie was able to recognize the dangers involved, then deduct from them the proper action to take.

"Give me a break! Who are they trying to kid? Dogs just aren't that intelligent!" I would always think to myself. But boy, did I have an epiphany headed my way...and it arrived in March of 1958.

The fateful day found my brother and me sitting together in the front yard. Shep had fully recovered from the snake bite of the previous October, and was there with us. What had attracted our attention was a crew of linemen who were busy repairing some overhead electrical cables at the corner of our yard. A severe ice storm, about a month earlier, had brought them down and they were just now being permanently repaired. In those days, the work was done much differently than it is today. Instead of being hoisted up to the work area on a truck-mounted "cherry picker," the repairmen had to scale the poles by using climbing belts, as well as steel gaffs buckled to the inside sole of their boots. Needless to say, Alvin and I were completely mesmerized by what we were watching.

The thing that fascinated us the most, was how easily the linemen were able to scale the pole. So after the crew had completed their work and left, we began having a discussion about it.

"It's real simple," I told my little brother. "The belt keeps them from falling, and they just use their feet to push themselves up the pole."

"No it don't!" Alvin answered right back. "They just hang their tools on the belt. It's them sharp things on their boots that get 'em up and down the pole!"

"Well, I betcha I can climb a pole without any old spikes on my shoes…just a belt around me and the pole!" I told him.

"No you can't, jelly head…and I dare you to try it!" came the ill-omened challenge.

"Oh no, he di'int!" I thought. We didn't actually talk like that back then, but I thought I'd throw that line in there for all the millennials reading this.

Never one to let a dare go unchallenged, I was determined to prove my younger brother wrong. I just needed to come up with a large enough belt…and I knew exactly where I could find one.

"I'll be back in a little while with a belt…then I'll show you!" I confidently stated.

Without taking time to thoroughly consider all of the possible repercussions, I was determined to prove to Alvin that I was right, and began running toward the house. After entering, I immediately felt a little more confident in my plan when I noticed that Mom was busy cleaning up the kitchen. I gave her a little nod and wave, which she returned with a curious look and a furrowed brow. Not wanting to arouse any more of her suspicion, I just scooted back around the corner and disappeared into my bedroom. Once I'd closed the door behind me, I walked over to the one to my right which led into my parents' bedroom. I then pressed my ear against it and listened closely.

"Zzzzzz...zzzzzz...zzzzzz," came the all too familiar sound... which was precisely what I was hoping for! Slowly, I pushed the door open. That is, until I was greeted by a rather loud "creeeeeeeeeeek!"

When that happened, I gritted my teeth and held the door right where it was. I knew if I closed it now, it'd only make that same sound again. And to my horror, the snoring abruptly stopped. My first impulse was to turn tail and run like a scared rabbit, but I'm afraid I was just a mite too stubborn to let a minor glitch like that stop me. Instead, I just stood there waiting for Dad's response, while desperately trying to come up with an excuse for interrupting his sleep, in case I needed one.

A cold sweat had already begun forming on my forehead when I, at last, heard a "cough...cough" come from my father. Then, I was mercifully granted a reprieve when the snoring suddenly began again. When I heard it, I quickly realized that if I were going to back out of this "fool's errand," now would be the time to do it. But no...I'd already come too far to give up now. Still yet, I was almost too scared to push on the door a second time. So I lifted up on it as I did and, much to my relief, it didn't make any more noise.

With a heightened sense of urgency, as well as newly found confidence, I began carefully tip-toeing across the darkened room.

My objective was a chair sitting in the far corner, just a few feet from the bed, and hanging over it was Dad's clothes. Of course, I was only interested in his pants, because that's where his belt would be. I was just about half way to the chair when another sudden and alarming "creeeeeeeeeeek" brought my mission to a literal standstill.

"Dad-burn it!" I thought to myself. "I knew that old loose board was there. I must've heard Mom and Dad step on it several thousand times going in and out of that room. But it's a little too late to remember it now. It looks like my "bacon is fried!"

"Who's in here?" I heard Dad shout in a somewhat slurred, sleep-addled voice.

Engulfed with fear, I just stood frozen in my tracks, waiting for the inevitable. It now looked as though I was going to get that old belt, after all...but in a much different manner than I had intended. Then, just as suddenly, came the welcoming "zzzzzz... zzzzzz...zzzzzz, once again."

"Whew!" came a sigh of relief, as I cautiously stepped away from the squeaky floor board. "Now, I'll just sloooowly back my way out of here, and count myself lucky. Then, we'll just forget all about this silly, little affair!"

If you guys believed that, then you didn't know me very well, did you? That belt was now only a few feet out of reach...and dang it, I'd already come too far to quit now!

Summoning my last ounce of audacity...or stupidity, depending on how you viewed the situation...I very tepidly took the remaining three steps, reached for Dad's pants and slid the belt out of the loops. Finally, with prize in hand, I quickly turned and snuck back out of the room. However, before leaving mine, I tucked the belt underneath my shirt in order to prevent Mom from discovering what I'd been up to. However, that in no way, shape or form prevented her from asking me about it!

"What's going on with you?" she inquired, just as I was about to open the front door.

"If I told you, I'd have to kill you," I dryly replied, before making a quick exit.

Now, do any of you think for a second that I really said that? Truthfully, Mom just looked at me kind of funny as I walked toward the door, without saying a word.

Once out the door, I began running around the house to the back yard, where I immediately collapsed to the ground behind the willow tree.

"Well, did you get it?" Alvin asked as I sat there gasping for air.

Without answering, I simply pulled Dad's belt from underneath my shirt and, with a sly smile, held it up.

"Good! I can't wait to see you fall off that pole," he responded with a smirk.

"Oh, I'm not gonna climb *that* pole," I corrected my brother, gesturing toward the front yard. "Mama would see me. But I know where there's a tree that'll work just the same."

The one I had in mind was a tall poplar sapling, which was limbless for quite a ways up the trunk…far enough for me to prove my point to Alvin. And it was located directly below our barn, which meant that it would be out of sight of the house.

There did happen to be one minor problem with that location, though. Well…maybe not minor. Okay, okay…it was a pretty major one! The tree just happened to be located inside the pasture fence…so it essentially belonged to Old Bess! But that was the only tree I knew of that would fulfill my purpose. And after what I'd just been through "appropriating" Dad's belt, I sure wasn't about to chicken out now.

So Alvin and I, with Shep tagging along, began making our way to the barn. However, before we could go inside the fence, Bess would need to be located. When I noticed her grazing contentedly at the other end of the pasture, just above the tree line, I turned to my brother and placed my finger over my lips. Then, after one more cautious glance toward the cow, we walked below the barn and squeezed between the strands of barbed wire.

Once inside the pasture, I led Alvin to the tree I had in mind, then positioned the belt around both my waist and the tree's slender trunk. Allowing just enough slack to be able to climb, I then buckled it securely in place. With an air of confidence, I leaned backward and began pushing myself upward with the inside soles of my high top sneakers. Once I'd gone a couple feet, I repositioned the belt and performed the same maneuver again. Slowly but steadily, I continued climbing up the tree until I reached several small limbs that impeded my progress. But I was confident that I'd gone high enough to prove my point, so I just looked down at my brother and proudly...but softly...let loose a victorious little, "Ta daaaaa!"

"Oh, you think you're so smart, butt hole!" an angry Alvin shouted at the top of his lungs.

Totally surprised and shocked by my brother's little temper tantrum, I quickly placed my finger over my lips and, this time, sent him a much louder, "sheeeeeeeeeesh!"

But I'm afraid my plea for silence was just a tad too late. Suddenly, an enraged bellow came echoing through the tree tops, followed closely by the sound of hoof beats thundering over the hard ground. Alvin heard it too, and began running as fast as his stubby, little legs would propel him toward the pasture fence.

When Bess reached the scene, she instantly turned in the direction of my brother, who could still be heard running through the dead, dry leaves. When that happened, I quickly tried to climb down and make my get away, too. But before I could descend more than a couple feet, the angry bovine wheeled back around in my direction, after seeing Alvin scoot, safely, under the fence.

With her anger unabated, Bess came charging directly to the sound of Shep's barking. There, she began a slow, threatening encirclement of the tree he was guarding. However, Shep bravely stood his ground, growling and snarling ferociously at her. Soon, a surreal and chilling scene began to materialize right before my eyes, as Bess would, intermittingly, stop her circling in order to paw the ground with her front hoof…after which, she would viciously jab at Shep with her lowered horns.

"Dang!" I thought to myself as I witnessed the bazaar drama unfold from my seemingly secure vantage point. "If that old cow had been born a bull somewhere in Spain, they'd have pictures of her covering the walls of every cantina in the country!" But then I felt it might be better if I applied my wild imagination to more constructive thoughts like, "How in the heck am I going to get my stupid butt out of this mess?"

"I know!" I thought. "Bess still doesn't know I'm up here, so I'll be real still and quiet, then, after a while, she'll just give up and go away. Yeah, that's the plan!"

But, apparently, I failed to pass along that game-winning strategy to my legs. After several minutes of being wrapped tightly around the slick tree trunk, they lost their grip and I went sliding back down it. When that happened, Bess looked straight up at me and let loose another angry bellow. Thank God, I was finally able to stop myself just a few inches from the business end of her horns. Then, like a scalded cat, I shifted my weary legs back into "climbing gear" and started back up the tree. But I'm afraid this wasn't entirely a good thing. For having come so close to skewering me like a shish kabab ready for the fire, only to see me get away at the last second, made Bess even more enraged!

Now, more determined than ever, she backed up several yards from the tree, then came charging toward it. Upon impact, it felt as though my teeth were about to fly out of my head! But when that failed to dislodge me, the big cow simply backed up and repeated the same tactic again…and again…and again. While this was going on, Shep was frantically barking and biting at Bess's legs. What a sight!

Overcome with terror, I began desperately breaking off the small branches that had previously prevented my upward progress, then climbed farther up the tree. Soon, I was so high that my weight caused the slender trunk to begin leaning toward the ground. At the time, I didn't regard this latest development as such a bad thing, because it meant that I no longer had to worry about sliding back down it. However, after a couple minutes of dangling in this precarious position, I suddenly came to the realization that I was stuck!

Adding to my dilemma, was the fact that Bess now saw that I was getting closer to the ground, which only encouraged her to ram the tree even harder. As this was taking place, the vibrations caused the belt to slip from my armpits, and begin sliding up my arms. I quickly realized there was nothing I could do about this situation, and the leather belt would eventually reach its inevitable stopping point…my scrawny, little neck!

Now, the only thing keeping me from becoming the next

"Tom Dooley" was a pair of tired legs locked precariously around the little tree. It quickly became apparent to me that unless I miraculously sprouted wings and flew away, this was one mess I'd gotten myself into that I wasn't getting out of. And when my legs, at last, lost their grip and I began swinging to and fro by my neck, a miracle was about the only thing that could possibly save me!

But not about to "go gentle into that good night," I grabbed the belt with both hands and tried with all my might to pull myself back up…but it was useless. As I felt the leather "noose" wind tighter and tighter around my neck, my last coherent thought was, "Butch, what in the heck have you gotten yourself into, this time?"

The conclusion of this little incident will have to be told from my mother's perspective, as she later related it to me. I'm afraid I was a little "hung up" at the time, and unable to recall what happened afterwards. So please bear with me.

My mother said she was still in the kitchen, and had just finished washing the breakfast dishes, when she heard Shep running toward the house barking frantically. Afraid he'd wake my father, she and Joan rushed to the back door to try to hush him up. However, by the time they got there, the highly agitated dog had already climbed to the top of the steps, and was now barking even louder.

"Shep, shut up!" Mama yelled, opening the door and swatting at him with her hand. But, to her shock, this only caused Shep to turn and run back down the steps, where he continued barking from the yard.

Not surprisingly, the commotion finally awakened Dad, and he was suddenly heard shouting from his bedroom, "Would somebody shut that damn dog up!"

"I'm trying to, Long...but he won't stop!" Mom shouted right back.

"Well, I sure as hell can make him stop!" my father angrily yelled, as he came rushing to the back door with a shoe in his hand.

Pushing past Mom, Dad furiously threw it at the barking dog, which only resulted in Shep deafly side-stepping the errant toss. However, gaining their attention appeared to be his desired goal, because Shep then turned and ran several yards towards the woods, before abruptly coming to a stop and running back.

When that happened, Mom yelled, "Shep, what's wrong?"

Seeming to understand what he was being asked, the dog again turned and ran toward the woods for a short distance, then stopped and looked back at Mom.

Turning to Dad, my mother said to him, "Long, I think he wants us to follow him. Something must be wrong with one of the boys!"

About this time, Alvin finally came walking, rather nonchalantly, back to the house.

"Where's your brother?" Dad gruffly asked him, which he answered with a simple arm motion toward the woods.

But that was enough for Mom, as she and Joan went rushing down the steps, followed by Dad. That is, as soon as he'd gone back to his bedroom for his other shoe. Then, the three of them began chasing after Shep, with my father trying to put the shoe on his foot, while holding up his drooping pants.

"Where's my damn belt?" he cursed, while pausing just long enough to gather up the shoe he'd thrown, and slip it on his foot.

When Bess saw my father approaching, she very judiciously vacated the scene, leaving only my limp, dangling body as evidence of what had taken place. By then, my face had turned a pale blue and my lips a morbid shade of purple…so for all practical purposes, it appeared that I was dead.

Evidently, the loud commotion hadn't gone unnoticed by the Greene sisters, who had been playing in their back yard. So, when they saw Mom, Dad and Joan running toward the woods, they surmised it was now safe enough for them to do the same. Mom later told me that, upon reaching the bazaar and frightening scene, the sisters began screaming, "Oh Lord! Oh Lord! Oh Lord!" at seeing me dangling by my neck from the tree."

Fortunately for me, Dad took a more hands-on approach to my predicament, and quickly began scaling the tree. But I'm afraid when he did, he was forced to let go of his trousers which, until then, he'd been holding up with one hand. Needless to say, they instantly dropped around his ankles when he started shimmying up the tree.

At this juncture in my story, I'm going to have to pause and warn you that the material you're about to read may be unsuitable for younger audiences, and may even be deemed offensive by some adults. Okay, just so we have that understood.

I probably should have brought this to your attention, earlier. But when I wrote that my father's trousers were hanging across the chair in his bedroom, I failed to mention that his boxer shorts were right there with them. It seems he had a small eccentricity in his sleeping habits. Ah heck, I'll just come right out and tell you. My father preferred doing it in the buff! *(buff: naked, nude, unclothed.)* And I suppose he was in too big of a hurry to bother putting them on with this deal going down. So, as you can imagine, when the ill-timed snafu occurred, the Greene sisters' "Oh Lord's" grew even louder.

Undeterred though, Dad somehow got to me and, with great effort, lifted my seemingly lifeless body just enough to remove the belt from around my neck. But, unfortunately, he wasn't able to climb back down carrying me, so his only option was to drop me to the ground. However, Mom alertly recognized this and came quickly to the rescue, holding out her arms…but, unfortunately, she missed.

Fortunately for me, though, that turned out to be a good thing! I landed flat on my back, knocking the "wind" back into my lungs, resulting in me miraculously regaining consciousness and gasping for air. After regaining more of my faculties, the first sensation I felt was Shep happily licking my face.

And I had also regained enough of my senses, by that time, to know that I probably should continue feigning death for as long as possible. Because I realized that if I got better too soon, the next contact I had with Dad's belt would be a little lower down on my anatomy!

Homeward Angel

I still remember that old story Dad told me. In fact, I'm sure I'll never forget it. It was the first time I wanted to cry at hearing of an animal's death. But this wasn't just an animal, it was a beloved pet…one that was deeply cared for, and dearly missed.

Sure, I'd seen the Walt Disney movie, *Old Yeller*, which appeared on our television about this same time. And I'm not ashamed to admit that I shed a few tears following its tragic ending, as anyone with half a heart would have done. However, in fairness, *Old Yeller* was just a movie, based on a book, which I'm fairly certain emanated solely from the fertile imagination of its author. But the story I'm about to tell you was an actual, real-life event, and it involved the very person who told it to me…my dad.

It seems my family was gathered together under the old willow tree in back of our house, one hot summer afternoon in 1958. The "culprit" that had brought us all together happened to be sitting directly in front of me, and I was staring disdainfully at it. It was a galvanized bushel tub. But that, in itself, wasn't what was drawing my ire. It was the fact that it was filled to the brim with freshly picked green beans…and it had really put a damper on what started out to be one of my better days!

This was a tedious and boring task my family performed, ritually, throughout the summer, along with shucking hundreds of ears of ripened corn, digging potatoes in the hot August sun and several other "goober" chores that allowed us to store our home-grown vegetables for winter use. But preparing our green beans for canning was the deal I hated most, simply because of the shear monotony of the work. Not only that, but it also played absolute havoc on one of my more important summertime activities… goofing off with Shep.

So in order to alleviate some of that monotony, and also make time pass a little faster, I looked forward…and only during these times, mind you…to some of Dad's old childhood stories. Especially, if they centered on the desperately hard times he experienced while growing up during the Great Depression of the 1930's. I guess the reason I liked to hear him tell these particular ones, is because they made what I was presently going through seem like child's play. And, besides, I'd already heard all of his war stories, which he seemed the most proud of. Briefly glancing down at Shep, who happened to be lying faithfully at my feet, I then turned my attention to Dad, just as Mom dropped a huge pile of freshly washed beans onto the newspaper I had placed in my lap.

"Daddy, I know your family kept huntin' dogs when you were a kid, but did you ever have a pet dog of your own?" I asked, hoping to get a conversation started.

Without looking up from the lap-full of beans he was expertly ridding of their course strings, and then breaking into inch and a half sections at an almost frantic pace, he muttered. "Hell no! We could barely afford to feed the ones that we used for huntin' game animals, so we could eat…let alone, a useless mutt. Heck, if I didn't kill a rabbit, or a squirrel or two…or maybe, sometimes a 'coon…I wouldn't have anything to eat at school the next day… 'cept maybe a biscuit, or a piece of cornbread."

I just stared at my father with a vacant expression, trying to comprehend the harsh reality of what he had just told me. Then, after quickly shaking my head back and forth several times, as if to snap myself from the trance his words had put me under, I calmly asked him, "So I take it you never had a pet, then?"

"Didn't say that," he almost growled, still not looking up from the task he was performing.

Puzzled and confused by Dad's half answer to my second question, I just sneered at him for a couple seconds, then in a demanding tone, blurted out, "Well, did you, or did you not, have a pet when you were growing up?"

Finally, my father looked up from the beans in his lap, and explained, "You asked me if I had a pet dog…and I didn't. But I guess I did have what some folks might consider to be a pet."

A tremendous feeling of excitement began to build at what Dad could possibly be talking about! However, I managed to tamp it back down a notch or two and lower my expectations, somewhat, when I thought about a more obvious, less exciting option for what my father was about to reveal.

"Please don't tell me you carried a frog around in your pocket, to scare little girls with!" I quipped, only half joking.

"Purty close! But I was a little more creative than that," he answered.

Completely pulled back in, but finally realizing that this was just one of those times my father wasn't in a talkative mood, I began to feel a little disappointment. However, I was still determined to get the story, even if I had to pry it out of him.

"Okaaay…is this something you'd like to share with us, or would you druther rehash one of them old warmed-over war stories we've all heard a hundred times?" I further goaded.

For the first time that afternoon, a smile appeared on Dad's face and he began telling this story:

"I reckon I was somewhere 'round your age, at the time," he began. "I'd been noticin' a pair of crows nestin' in a big white pine tree in back of our house. I'd heard folks tellin' stories 'bout how smart they were, and figgered one of 'em might make a good pet. So I kept a watch on the tree for the next couple weeks or so, 'till I noticed 'em carryin' food to the nest. It was then that I knew the chicks had hatched."

Dad paused just long enough to reach for the pack of cigarettes in his pocket and light one, then continued with his story.

"I waited 'bout a week after that. Then, one mornin', I decided it was time to climb the tree. The nest was all the way up at the top, and when I got about half way up it, the parents started atackin' me! But I wasn't about to stop after climbin' that far, so I kept goin'. Purty soon there were dozens of 'em comin' after me…just a swoopin' down, peckin' and clawin'. I'd always heard that the whole flock would take care of one another, and come to the rescue if one of 'em got in trouble...and boy, they sure did!

But I kept on climbin', and when I finally made it to the nest, I had peck marks all over my arms and face. So I just reached in and grabbed the biggest chick, put him in the feed sack that I had tucked inside my overalls, then started back down the tree.

Now, don't you know, that made 'em even madder, so I started climbin' down so fast that limbs and bark were flyin' everywhere. My feet kept losing traction and I almost fell a couple times, but I finally made it to the ground in one piece."

"But did the chick?" I asked, with my mouth wide open.

"Yeah, he survived it just fine," Dad answered.

"Well, what did you do with him?" was my next question.

Dad hesitated for several seconds, I'm sure to refresh his memory, then responded, "Oh, I found an old shoebox somewhere, punched a few holes in the lid, and kept him in there 'til I could build a bigger cage out of sawmill slabs and discarded window screen."

"How in the heck did you keep him alive?" I asked, becoming completely enthralled in Dad's story. "I mean it's not like you could go just anywhere and pick up an instruction manual on raising a wild, baby crow!"

"Oh, I'd seen plenty of birds takin' care of their young to sorta know what to do," he answered. "So I started out feedin' him small pieces of bread. Then, every once in a while, I'd give him one soaked in water. But when he got a little bigger, I'd just toss him the entrails of the fish and game we cleaned. Shoot, it wouldn't no time at all 'til he was eatin' the same stuff I was."

"Did you always keep him in that cage you built for him?" I then asked, with my curiosity reaching fever pitch.

"Oh, heck no," Dad replied. "As soon as he got big enough to fly, I started takin' him outside and throwin' him up in the air. It wouldn't long at all 'til he was flyin' from tree to tree. After that, I trained him to fly to my arm when I'd hold it out. Then, I just started leavin' him outside all the time, and whenever I'd come out of the house, he'd foller me around, flyin' to wherever I'd go."

"Wow!" was all I could say as I just sat there with my mouth agape for several seconds, trying to imagine how neat it must have felt to have a pet that unique and different.

Finally awakening from my self-induced "coma," I then asked Dad the question I was the most curious about, "What the heck did you name him?"

When Dad responded with, "Blackie," a long pause followed while I just sat staring at him with, I'm sure, an obvious scowl.

"How original!" I finally replied, making sure he noticed the conspicuous eye roll that accompanied my backhanded compliment.

But in fairness, I did have to admit to myself, "What would be a better name for a crow?"

It was about this time that Dad glanced over at the large pile of unbroken green beans still remaining in my lap and chided, "If you'd git them fingers moving 'bout half as fast as your mouth, we might not have stay out here the rest of the damn evenin'."

With my father's crude admonishment ringing in my ears, I revved my engine up a notch or two, but still remained just as honed in on his story. So after only a short stretch of working at my newly discovered pace, I slowed back down just a little to get in one final question.

"How long did you have Blackie…and what became of him?" I meekly queried. Yeah, I know…that was two, but I was afraid Dad would lose patience with me again.

And I'll never forget how he just stared directly at me for several titillating seconds…but not really at me. It was almost as though he was looking through me. Thinking back on it now, I guess it took him a little while to brush the cobwebs from those old memories. Then, much to my relief, Dad finally started back telling his story.

"I guess it was somewhere 'round the last of March when I got him, and I still had him when school started back up in September. So I'm thinkin' it was probably toward the end of that month when it happened."

I couldn't believe it when my father interrupted his incredible saga right there, and got up to empty his finished beans into the large canning pot. If not for the fact that I was sitting on the ground, I'm positive I would have been teetering on the edge of my seat! With what felt like pins and needles pricking my body, I just watched as he pulled several more handfuls of beans from the bushel tub and piled them onto his newspaper. I was still watching him with eyes wide open when he sat down and went back to work. Thankfully, Joan bailed me out and asked him the appropriate, follow-up question, "Well Daddy, what did happen to him?"

"Blackie would always go with me to the old school house that I had to walk 'bout six miles to every mornin' when school was underway, then wait for me in a nearby tree 'til it let out," Dad stated, finally continuing his story. "Oh, he would fly off a few times to get food and water, but he was always there when I came out at the end of the school day to foller me back home."

I'm fairly certain that by this stage of Dad's story, there were a lot of my peeled strings finding their way into the broken bean pot…and vice versa…as I became more and more engrossed in his fascinating tale. So much so, that I almost felt that I had become a part of it. And I'm sure the reason he was being so deliberate in his "slow roll" telling of it, was to get back at me for giving him "grief" over his war stories. But whatever he was up to, Dad had captured my undivided attention, as he continued on.

"We were on our way home one day when I decided to stop by the old general store that was located 'bout half way between the school and our house," he recounted. "I had helped my dad cut a load of pulpwood the Saturday before, and take it to the lumber mill in Marion, for sale. The little bit of money I had earned was burnin' a hole in my pocket. And all day long, my mind had been on the big jar of hard candy I always stared at whenever I was there, but couldn't afford to buy.

It was a purty warm day, so the front door had been left open. When I walked in, Blackie flew right in behind me and lit on the counter. The lady storekeeper didn't know what to think, so she grabbed a broom and started swingin' it at him. Then I started hollerin' at her, tryin' to tell her that that was my crow. By the time she stopped swingin', Blackie had flown back out the door. So I bought the candy I'd been hankerin' for and walked back outside. When I didn't see Blackie around anywhere, I figgered the lady had scared the daylights out of him, and he'd flown on to the house ahead of me. But when I got there, he was nowhere to be found."

"Long, I've heard this story before!" Mom suddenly interrupted. "Do you really think it's something you oughta be telling the kids?"

"Well, I sure do!" I hastily blabbered out, much to Mom's chagrin.

Quickly realizing my place, I then meekly explained, "Uh…I mean…well, don't you think he's done got into a little too far to stop now?"

"Yeah, I guess I have…and besides, you'd never stop pesterin' me about it," Dad said, glancing over at Mom who just looked down at her work and shook her head. Seeing that she wasn't going to raise any further objections, Dad leaned back in his chair a little, looked directly at me and continued.

"I just walked 'round the house, and all about, makin' crow sounds," he began explaining. You know, 'Caw! Caw! Caw!' like I always did when I wanted him to come to me, but I couldn't find him anywhere. So finally, not knowin' what else to do, I just sat down on the front steps, thinkin' sooner or later he'd turn up.

Then 'bout sundown, I noticed something small kinda hoppin' along up the dirt road leadin' to the house. Our chickens hadn't gone to their roosts yet, and were still gathered about in the front yard. So before I could make out what it was in the fadin' light, it disappeared right into the middle of 'em. When it finally came out, I could tell that it was Blackie, but he was holdin' one of his wings kinda down and out to the side. And it didn't take a rocket surgeon to figger out what had happened to him. That dern lady storekeeper had busted his wing with her damn broom! I was just about to jump to my feet and go runnin' to get Blackie, when our big ole rooster beat me to him. The son-of-a-gun jumped on my crow and started floggin' the heck out of him! By the time I got there to put a stop to it, Blackie was dead."

For a brief moment after my father finished depicting this disturbing, yet tender, narrative, he just seemed to gaze off into the distance with a blank expression…then, released an audible sigh and quickly went back to working on the beans in his lap. Mom's expression, however, was far from blank, when she noticed the tears that had gathered in my sister's eyes, and saw me simply drop my head in reverend silence at that poor crow's undeserved fate.

Though I didn't see it, I could just imagine the cold, hard

stare she was giving my father, as everyone just suddenly fell silent, including me. But although my lips had uncharacteristically stopped moving, my mind was churning furiously.

My first thought was; would my father not have been much better off had he just left the baby crow in its nest that day...and avoided all the grief and heartbreak he surely experienced, watching a beloved pet die such a tragic death?

Then, my thoughts shifted to the crow's perspective. Wouldn't he have been much better off, also, had he been allowed to be raised and cared for by his parents? Certainly, he would've stood a much better chance of living a longer, more normal life.

Still in deep contemplation, I glanced down at Shep, who had remained at my feet the whole time, and found my answer. "No!" A resounding, "No!"

Even though I realized that sometime in the future, I would have to face the same sad day of reckoning with Shep that my father had faced with Blackie, there's no way I'd turn the clock back and dismiss him from my life, even if I could. If I allowed that to happen, I never would've experienced the special and peculiar bond a dog exhibits toward a human...an almost sacred covenant that forever binds the two together.

And not only dogs, many other types of animals display this same interspecies connection with man. After all, Blackie, a simple, little crow, hopped three miles with a broken wing to get back to my father, because he loved him that much. This was the same fealty and devotion Shep had demonstrated to me, time after time...and under circumstances that could even have cost him his life!

I guess what I'm trying to say is; when, and if, a treasure so rare and priceless happens to wander into your life, you don't look back down the road to make sure there's no pain and heartache following along behind it. You just thankfully accept and embrace it for what it is, in that moment, for it may never come along again.

I was suddenly shaken from my thoughts by Dad's, "If you don't stop piddlin' around with those beans again, you'll be out here workin' with nothing but the porch light!"

With that, I threw it back into high gear and began working furiously on the remaining beans in my lap. I also tried to put Dad's story out of my mind…well, at least, the sadder details of it…for today wasn't a day to be melancholy, not after the great news I had gotten the day before.

But even before that, I had begun noticing signs that conditions regarding my physical infirmities may be on an upward trajectory…for the better. It had started out with little things that, at the time, I didn't attach a lot of importance to. Then later, I began noticing that Dad wasn't constantly harping at me to straighten up and stop drooping my shoulders. And just before my last visit to the clinic, he had me stand with my back against a half open door, to check my posture. On that occasion, unlike all the prior ones, there wasn't the usual, "Not much improvement. I guess we're gonna have to work even harder."

So you can imagine my relief when this come-to-be-expected reaction was surprisingly replaced with, "Not too bad. Sue, come here and take a look."

And when Mom did, all of my hard work was made more than worthwhile! After observing how much straighter my back fit against the door, she gave me a hug and exclaimed, "That looks so much better! Son, I'm so proud of you!"

Then, in a little aside comment meant only for me, she

lowered the volume of her voice slightly, while further stating, "In all honesty, I'd been noticing a lot of improvement lately, but didn't want to mention it to you until your next visit to the clinic, to make sure the doctor agrees."

And her observations were confirmed the next day, after the doctor had me remove my shirt. He then made several slow circles around me, while closely studying my posture. I just stood there, erect as a statue, as this was taking place. Finally, he stopped directly in front of me and crossed his arms. For a second or two, I didn't know how to react when the doctor suddenly extended his right arm to me. After finally realizing what his intention was, I quickly did the same.

As we stood there shaking hands, he smiled and said, "Well Butch, it's been a real pleasure working with you. But I'm happy to say that we won't be seeing any more of one another, after today...and I mean that in a good way!"

The doctor then turned to my father and further stated, "In all my years of working with children suffering from post-polio muscle atrophy, I've never seen a case where it was reversed to this extent...not even close.

Our trip back home was kind of unprecedented, also. The whole time, Dad just gripped the steering wheel tightly with both hands, while belting out his "cover" of Ernest Tubb's *Walking The Floor Over You,* which was typical of him when he was in a good mood. But this time, I didn't seem to mind, even though I wasn't all that crazy about the original version. I just sat there and smiled the whole time. However, I will admit that I was more glad than usual when the car finally turned into our driveway.

And my smile grew even wider when Shep came running to greet me, as I was getting out of the car. I quickly knelt to embrace him, while shouting, "We did it, Boy!"

For the next couple weeks, my days just seemed to fly delightfully by, without a care in the world…and that was something I hadn't experienced in almost four years. Ever since that last visit to the clinic, it seemed as though a heavy burden had been lifted from my shoulders. I had discovered a new spring in my step, as well as a totally changed and improved outlook on life. Everything was, seemingly, going great.

That is, until that Fourth of July day rolled around, only a short while later. There was something that just didn't seem right, from the very moment I awoke that morning. I don't know how to describe it, other than this weird feeling in the pit of my stomach…sort of a surreal sensation of impending doom that I'd never felt before. Sure, I'd certainly had plenty of recent experience with troubled and worrisome thoughts. However, this was much different. What I was feeling, that particular day, seemed more immediate and urgent.

But I tried hard to push all of those bad thoughts aside, and stop worrying so much about things I had no control over. Besides, it was probably nothing more than a few residual effects from all the anxiety and concern I'd been forced to deal with, throughout the past several years.

Now, thankfully, a new day had dawned. The *Sword of Damocles* that had swung so perilously over my head, had been dislodged and locked away forever. The demons that had been lurking in the dark abysses of my mind, waiting to spring forth and attack me whenever I allowed myself to think happy thoughts about my future, had, likewise, been excommunicated from it and banished to some faraway place. The door to my very soul had been flung open, and all the dark angels that had been dwelling there had gone flying out, screeching and screaming, never to return. My problem now was simply learning how to deal with this new reality, and, so far, I wasn't doing a very good job of it.

Anyway, I didn't have time to think about any of that stuff, so I tried to block it from my mind. This wasn't the time to conjure up my old demons from the past...not today. It was the Fourth of July and a whole bunch of my uncles, aunts and cousins were coming over to celebrate it with my family. So I needed to get myself busy thinking about that, instead.

You know, looking back on it now, I have no idea what compelled me to start digging that hole. It could've been an old pirate movie I had recently watched, where the "swashbucklers" dug a secret hole to bury their looted treasure in, but I've no actual recollection of it. What I definitely do recall, however, is watching my Uncle Calvin and his two oldest sons, Bo and Mack, digging a new well to replace the old one that had gone dry. Alvin and Dean watched this with me, also, as we were too young to participate in such a dangerous endeavor.

At first, we were a little miffed that we weren't allowed to help them out, although I realize now that my uncle was just looking out for our safety. But at the time, it just seemed that my cousin, my brother and I were missing out on a lot of fun. I guess that's why I came up with the idea to dig a hole of our own...one they had absolutely no control over.

It didn't take a lot of coaxing to get the other two to participate in the venture with me. So, after picking out a spot on the extreme northern boundary of our property, and about half way down...then, covertly confiscating a shovel and mattock from the barn, we were soon busy gouging out a crater in the dry, hard-packed dirt. However, not long into the travail, Alvin and Dean decided that maybe what they had witnessed earlier in the day wasn't much of a game, after all.

After watching kind of disdainfully as my brother and cousin moved on to less arduous activities, I continued digging the hole. Of course, Shep wasn't about to desert me, so he sat down nearby and intently observed. It soon became an obsession with me, and I didn't stop until almost dark. After going to bed that night, I think I even dreamed about the hole, and couldn't wait to get started on it again when I arose the next morning.

It was about four foot square and four feet deep, when Dad finally discovered what I was doing…and I knew he eventually would. But interestingly enough, he didn't try to stop me.

"Just what the heck do you think you're doing, boy?" he asked, after walking down to where I was laboring.

Looking up at him while wiping the sweat from my brow, I simply replied, "Diggin' a hole."

With that, I paused what I was doing, leaned on my shovel and kind of grimaced at what I knew was coming next. So I was a little surprised when Dad calmly responded with, "Well, make sure you put that shovel and mattock back where you got 'em… after you git to Chiner."

Trying unsuccessfully to keep from snickering as he walked away, I quickly went back to work. I guess he figured what I was doing was good exercise, so he sure wasn't about to interfere with it…especially, as difficult as it had been to get me to exercise in the past.

So, when my cousins were gathered about on the holiday I had begun describing, I couldn't wait to take some of the boys down to see what I'd been doing, as I was pretty proud of it. Needless to say, they were somewhat less impressed, and asked what in the world would compel me to dig such a big hole in the ground. And for the first time, I had to ask myself the same question, "Why did I dig it?"

After running that baffling enigma through my mind for several seconds, the only answer I was able to come up with, was the very one I gave them, "I don't know. For some strange reason, I just felt like digging a hole."

It was about this time, Mom yelled out that dinner was ready. But while my cousins were running back toward the house, I just kept standing there, staring down at the hole. Finally, I was jarred from my thoughts when I felt Shep brush against my leg. I knelt down to take him in my arms, and he too looked down at it, then raised his head back up and began licking the side of my face.

Later that afternoon, when dinner was over with and most of the guests had left, my family and a few holdovers were gathered in the backyard, under the old willow. Dad had carried a large watermelon from the basement, and was just getting ready to slice it. But as I was sitting with my back to the tree, anticipating the delicious treat headed my way, Shep, who had been lying between my legs, suddenly stood and began licking my face, once again. When I started affectionately stroking his head, he looked me directly in the eyes for several seconds, before walking toward the corner of the house. I called for him to return, and for the first time since we'd been together, he purposely disobeyed my command and kept walking.

Puzzled by his strange behavior, I rose to my feet and followed after him. When I reached the side of the house and saw him walking down the driveway, toward the road, I once again called for him…and he once again ignored my command. Upon reaching the road, he sat down on his haunches, then turned one last time to look at me.

It looked harmless enough when I first noticed it coming down the highway. That same blue and white, '55 Oldsmobile, driven by that same elderly, gray-haired lady. I had seen it pass our house numerous times, never going more than forty miles an hour, about the speed she was driving it then. And I know Shep saw it coming, too. Because he turned his head and looked up the road right at it…then walked directly in front of it.

If I were to live to be a thousand, I know I'll never hear a sound so horrific. Just as I know I'll never forget it...the two seconds of squealing tires, followed immediately by the loud thud of impact. When I heard it, I dropped limply to my knees and tried to scream, "Shep!" But no words could escape my mouth.

I was still on my knees when Dad came running by me. When he reached Shep's blood-soaked body, he just looked down at him, then at me, and shook his head. By this time, the lady had gotten out of her car and was walking toward the scene, while profusely apologizing, "I'm sorry! I'm so sorry!" But no one blamed her.

All I remember after that, was Mom walking up behind me and tenderly placing her hands on my shoulders…and Joan kneeling down beside me, sobbing uncontrollably. I tried to cry, too, but the intense state of shock that had suddenly overcome me, wouldn't allow it.

When I saw my father lift Shep's body from the road and begin carrying him toward the northern boundary of our property, I immediately knew where he was being taken…to the grave Shep had watched me dig for him.

As I was about get to my feet and go help, I felt added pressure from Mom's hands on my shoulders, and heard her softly say, "You don't want to see that. You'll want to remember him the way he was."

And I knew she was right. So instead, I quickly rose to my feet and went running to the house, and into my bedroom, where I began to cry…and cry…and cry.

For the rest of that evening and deep into the night, I prayed for God to command the earth to stop turning on its axis… to somehow prevent the sun from rising on a new day. Then I wouldn't have to face the morning light, knowing Shep would no longer be waiting at the door to greet me.

The Repayment

Of course, it did rise…as I knew it would. But that didn't mean I had to get out of bed and go walking out that door…at least, not yet. It was as though I could avoid the added heartache that would involve, if I just remained in my bed. So I was determined to stay in it for eternity…and was doing a pretty good job of it, when I finally heard the bedroom door open. It was Mom. She walked over and sat down next to where I was lying, then gently placed her hand on my forehead.

"Butch, you really should try to get up," she said. "You've been in here since six o'clock yesterday evening, and it's almost nine now."

I just looked up at her through swollen, tear-stained eyes and softly replied, "I don't want to get up, Mama. I just can't."

"Well, I made your favorite breakfast, pancakes…and I'm keeping them warm for you. So you try to get yourself up," she pleaded.

"I'll try, Mama, but I don't think I can…and I know I can't eat anything," was all I was able to say, before rolling over and burying my face in my pillow.

As my muted sobs, once again, began filling the room, Mom got up to leave, then sat back down.

"Son, I just want you to know that you're not the only one hurting right now," she said in her most soothing voice, while tenderly stroking the back of my head. "Even though the rest of us weren't as close to Shep as you were, we still loved him…and we've all cried. I even noticed some tears in your father's eyes after he came back from burying him."

Mom then paused for a moment to collect herself, and when she resumed I noticed a discernible breaking in her voice.

"Long and I were even talking, last night, about what a sad little boy you were before Shep came along, and how much you've changed these past three years…inside and out. He made you happy again, so it would be a darn shame if you went back to the way you were, and let everything Shep did for you, be for nothing. So you think about that!" she was finally able to tell me.

After Mom left the room, I did exactly that. I stopped crying and began thinking about all the wonderful things Shep had done for me. Everything we had experienced together and all that we'd gone through, good and bad, began racing through my mind. For the next hour my brain became an open vessel, capturing each and every memory in vivid detail, then locking them away deep inside its many crevices and fissures, never to be forgotten.

Once this process had been completed, I rolled over onto my back, and for the first time that morning, noticed the bright sunshine that was flowing through my window. As I just lay there watching the tiny particles of dust dancing about in the bright rays, one more thought entered my mind…a bittersweet one.

Even though I would never see Shep again, or feel his touch, he would always be with me. After all, how could something that was loved so much ever go away?

Finally forcing myself into a sitting position, I was rubbing my eyes when the door opened again.

"Oh, good! I was just coming to get you!" Mom exclaimed, seeming much more cheerful than when she last spoke to me. "There's something you've just got to see! I know it'll make you feel better."

"Well, what is it?" I asked, shakily getting to my feet.

Mom's smile grew even wider, as she began to explain, "Your friends have been coming by the house all morning, and going down to Shep's grave. I finally walked down there and…well, you'll just have to go see it for yourself."

"Mama, I don't think I'm ready for that…not yet, anyway," I replied, with tears, once again, welling up in my eyes.

"Well, you can stay in the house all day, feeling sorry for yourself, or walk down there and face your pain, head on. You never know, it just might take some of your hurting away," Mom advised me. "I'll leave the decision up to you. But Son, I really do think you should go down there."

When Mom left my room, I drew a long, deep breath then slowly released it. I realized that, sooner or later, I would have to deal with the fact that Shep was no longer in my life…and the longer I put off dealing with it, the more I would hurt. Still yet, I would rather have taken a thousand beatings than to walk outside, knowing he wouldn't be running to greet me.

When I finally gathered enough courage to do what I knew I must, I still had to allow for one minor deviation. Normally, I would exit the house through the front door, but this time I went out the back one, instead. I knew Shep's sleeping mat would be laying on the front porch, beneath my window, and I just wasn't quite ready to confront it. And I wasn't ready for what awaited me at the bottom of those steps, either. That late morning, mid-summer day I was about to enter into, was like nothing I'd ever witnessed before…or since.

As I began walking in the direction of the grave, though my head was still numb and throbbing from all the crying I had done, it felt as though my senses were no longer confined by my body. I don't know of a way to describe the feeling, other than, for some strange reason, my mind seemed much more attuned to everything around me than it normally did. All of the flowers and blossoms surrounding our house looked more colorful and vibrant, and smelled more fragrant than I ever remembered. Even the grass seemed greener, and the chirping of the birds and the buzzing of the insects sounded more clear and audible than ever before. And although it was a relatively warm day, even the very air I was walking through felt less humid and more refreshing than it normally did for that time of year.

But even as extraordinary as all of these conditions were, they paled in comparison to what I witnessed upon coming in sight of Shep's grave. For piled high on it, were dozens of homemade wreaths and bouquets of flowers. Flowers, of every hue and color, picked from the neighborhood yards, or gathered wild from the surrounding fields.

Still in disbelief at what I was seeing, I walked over and sat down next to the grave. After several minutes of admiring the beauty in front of me, I began talking to Shep. I just wanted to let him know that the many amazing and courageous acts he'd performed, during his short time on earth, hadn't gone unappreciated by me, or unnoticed by others. For the multitude of flowers that had been gathered and brought there, was certainly proof of the latter. But mostly, I just wanted to thank him for the life he saved and returned to me. And as it had been for him, when it came my time to leave the mortal boundaries of this earth, he'd be the last thought on my mind.

Then after a few minutes of silent reflection, the question that had been gnawing so viciously at me, just had to be asked.

"Why? Why, Shep?" I asked in an almost pleading voice, while staring down at the grave. "You always seemed to know when my life was in danger. Surely, you understood what would happen when you walked in front of that car. Why?"

There was something beautiful, and at the same time, mysterious about that little black and purple butterfly, as I watched it appear to just float down from out of the clear blue and alight on a bouquet of still fresh daisies. For a short period, it remained in place, fluttering its shimmering wings slowly back and forth, as it fed on the sweet, succulent nectar still contained in the flowers. Then, as mysteriously as it had come, it suddenly propelled itself upward and began to fly farther and farther into the beautiful Carolina blue sky, until it finally disappeared against a backdrop of puffy, white cumulous clouds.

Have you ever experienced a "eureka moment?" I'm sure you know what I'm talking about. One of those times when you've been racking your brain over a problem that appeared unsolvable, or maybe the meaning of a strange set of circumstances that happened to you, and never being quite able to figure it out. Then, something seemingly insignificant occurs, and all of a sudden the solution to the riddle becomes as obvious as the nose on your face. Well, I just had my first!

It was never any type of coincidence that caused Shep to mysteriously turn up at my house, that cold November morning. An eight-week old puppy that had been brought to a new home, only a few days earlier, wouldn't just suddenly decide that he preferred the house a quarter of a mile down the road, one that he knew nothing about...and a home in which one of the occupants needed him so badly. Then, after repeated attempts by his rightful owners to take him back, to keep returning, time after time, even when it meant going to extraordinary lengths to do so.

And even if all of those things could somehow be reconciled, how could one ever account for the numerous times Shep saved my life, by just happening to be in the right place at the right time? I guess maybe one could argue that this was nothing more than a series of fortuitous happenstances, but that would require stretching the limits of reason to the breaking point. No, in my mind, it was now as clear as that bright July day, that Shep wasn't just a dog...but rather, an angel, who had been sent to me on an earthly mission. Then, upon the successful completion of that mission, had been called back home.

After all, if the vast majority of the world's population possessed the presumptiveness to believe in an omnipotent God... one who commanded the power to steer the world in any direction he desired, as well as grant requests to all mortals he deemed worthy, then who could possibly fault me for believing that, in this particular incidence, he did just that?

A short time after all these childhood revelations, as described in my adult vocabulary, had been thoroughly absorbed into my brain, my mother suddenly appeared at the grave site and sat down next to me.

"I can't believe all the trouble they went through to do this for me," I told Mom as she placed her arm around me. "Somebody must've told them how hard I was taking it."

"Oh, I don't think they did it just for you," Mom replied. "And it didn't seem like it was any trouble when I was watching them carrying all those flowers down here. I think it was just something they wanted to do."

"Well, I sure appreciate it…and I'm sure Shep does, too," I responded.

After a few more minutes of silent contemplation, I was finally ready to return to the house. As Mom and I were walking back, side by side, I turned around for one final look, then gazed up at the sky, in the direction the little butterfly had flown.

"Mama, you were right. I do feel a lot better now," I told her.

Although I was given the answer to the "Why" that day, it seems I've been struggling ever since with the "Why me?" After all, it's not like I've accomplished anything earth-shattering in life, since the time this strange saga unfolded. Then, with each successive disappointment and failure, the "Why me?" only grew louder and harder to understand.

Now, to be perfectly honest, I'd always felt a strong compulsion to write a book depicting these events, and thought maybe that could possibly be the purpose behind it all. However, if that were the case, I couldn't figure out how to write the book without it becoming an autobiography. Shep certainly deserved to be written about, but I sure didn't.

Then, a tragic event occurred that changed everything. My grandson, Ayden, whom I'd spent a lot of time with, and who loved dogs and other animals every bit as much as me, died in a horrible accident. When it happened, he was only nine years old, the same age I was when Shep died. And it occurred on my sixtieth birthday. Then, to make this terrible tragedy even more bewildering and heartbreaking, he accidently hanged himself while playing in a tree…the same fate that should have befallen me, had it not been for Shep.

As you can imagine, this dreadful accident, combined with the many similar circumstances and bewildering links, caused the "Why me?" to return even stronger and more intense. For several years afterward, the terrible clinical depression I'd dealt with, ever since my struggles with polio, became almost unbearable.

So, although I still felt compelled to write this book, to pay homage to an extraordinary dog that had performed many amazing deeds, Ayden's death made it even harder for me to understand what meaning the book could possibly convey. I remained convinced that Shep had been sent to me by some divine force, and his actions had been guided by that same power, but the reason why had become impossible for me to comprehend.

Then one night, during a period of fitful sleep, I dreamt that I was talking to Ayden.

"Pawpaw, please write the book!" he began pleading with me.

"Ayden, I can't write the book, because I don't know how to end it," I answered back.

"But you told me all of those great stories about Shep, stories that lots of other people would love to hear. So please, Pawpaw, write the book!" he again urgently requested.

"Ayden, Shep was hit by a car and died," I responded in the dream. "Lots of dogs have died that way, so the book would only be a jumbled up bunch of childhood memories that no one would want to read about."

All I remembered after that was him smiling sweetly, then

saying to me, "Pawpaw, you write the book and let the ending take care of itself."

Still asleep, my grandson's image began to slowly fade from my dream, until I awoke with a thud. Bolting upright in bed, I began grabbing for my clothes, while shouting aloud, "Jesus Christ! If it means that much to him, then I'll write the darn book!"

During the next several weeks, I worked almost nonstop trying to repay that long overdue debt. And you know what? Ayden was right! The ending did take care of itself. When I started writing, I put no thought into how I would end this book. Then, just when I got to these last two pages, a thought struck my brain as powerfully as a bolt of lightning, bringing about my second "eureka moment."

This book isn't about me, and it's not entirely about a dog… but rather, a message. A profound and heartfelt one, inspired by the exploits and devotion of a remarkable animal, and witnessed by a young boy who was blessed with just enough God-given ability to later document it in writing.

Then, incredibly, words began streaming from my mind and onto the tips of my fingers at such a tremendous pace, I couldn't type them fast enough. It felt as though I had come under some type of divine intervention that was running the words directly through me and transcribing them onto my computer screen. Once completed, this is what that message became:

To never give up searching for life's purpose and meaning, even when confronted by obstacles that appear overwhelming and insurmountable. When we persevere and eventually overcome them, we earn a greater reward than had we never faced them at all.

To never underestimate the power of love. When given

unconditionally, even a creature as simple and humble as a crow is capable of returning it tenfold.

To never mourn the contents of a grave without first noticing the bouquets of flowers that adorn its top, and realize the love, admiration and respect that caused them to be there.

That sometimes the answers to some of life's most complicated and perplexing riddles can be found on something as unexpected and fragile as the wings of a butterfly, if we only bother to look.

That time isn't some inanimate object with a value that is determined by the amount we have in our possession, or the total sum of it that we had to spend. But instead, a living, breathing energy that grows and expands, proportionately, by how much it is cherished.

And finally, never expect a prayer to be answered in some preconceived way or timetable. It may not be answered when or how we want it to be. It may not be answered in the here and now. And it may not even be answered at all. But if it ever is, one thing is for certain; it will never be answered by a heavenly creature adorned in a flowing, white robe and bourn about on celestial wings.

Therefore, never lose hope. Instead, keep searching for answers in unexpected places and mysterious ways. For who's to know what form an angel will take when it's heaven sent.

Lightning Source UK Ltd.
Milton Keynes UK
UKHW020653131020
371498UK00013B/521

9 781977 231611